Preface

Mental retardation is a many-faceted national problem that involves diverse disciplines, ranging from health care to education, and impinges on social and political policy. For the individual and the family, mental retardation presents very practical concerns. For the community, state, and nation, it presents educational, social, economic, and political challenges.

It is estimated that nearly 3% of newborn infants will be diagnosed as mentally retarded at some time during their lives. However, this figure probably represents a substantial overdiagnosis, because it includes cases of "functional retardation," particularly among the poor; cases of "minimal cerebral dysfunction"; and cases of learning and emotional disorders. It is likely that the true incidence of mental retardation is less than 1% of the population in the United States.

Diagnostic difficulties also hamper incidence studies. While measuring intelligence is relatively easy, diagnosis of mental retardation requires consideration of impairment in adaptation, a much more difficult aspect to quantify.

Only during the school years do general adaptation and measured intelligence correlate to a high degree, since the major expectation of school-aged children is academic performance. Therefore, many retarded children--particularly the mildly impaired from low socioeconomic groups--may become clinically visible only upon entering school and may again become asymptomatic in adulthood.

Far-reaching changes in social policy have occurred since publication of the first AMA handbook on mental retardation in 1965. At that time, few alternatives to institutional care existed. Now various options are available, ranging from care in the individual's home to settings in the community, such as foster homes and small residential facilities.

Accompanying this shift has been legislation addressing related issues (eg, the right of mentally retarded persons to care in the least restrictive setting; allocation of funds for their treatment, education, and employment).

These social changes have paralleled major scientific advances. For example, certain screening tests have almost completely eliminated the type of mental retardation caused by phenylketonuria. Genetic counseling and testing have prevented or averted other types of retardation and birth defects. The implication of modifiable risk factors (eg, maternal alcohol use, smoking) in some disorders may lead to changes in lifestyle that result in a reduced incidence of mental retardation. And the treatment of certain maladaptive disorders with behavioral management and psychotropic drugs has resulted in better care for many retarded patients.

This handbook serves as an introduction to clinical issues surrounding mental retardation and provides an overview of services and resources available to mentally retarded individuals. Although it is not a textbook about mental retardation, it contains important material that may be helpful to practicing physicians as well as to medical students, nurses and nursing students, psychologists, sociologists, social workers, educators, social and political planners, and the families of mentally retarded persons.

The physician's perspective will be emphasized because, in many cases, he or she is the only health professional who has contact with every family member early in the mentally retarded child's life. The physician can identify the child as retarded years before a diagnosis might otherwise be made by other health professionals or teachers, and management can be initiated to modify the course of the disorder. Early identification is particularly important in cases of mental retardation associated with psychosocial disadvantage, where enrichment of the

AMA Handbook On
MENTAL RETARDATION

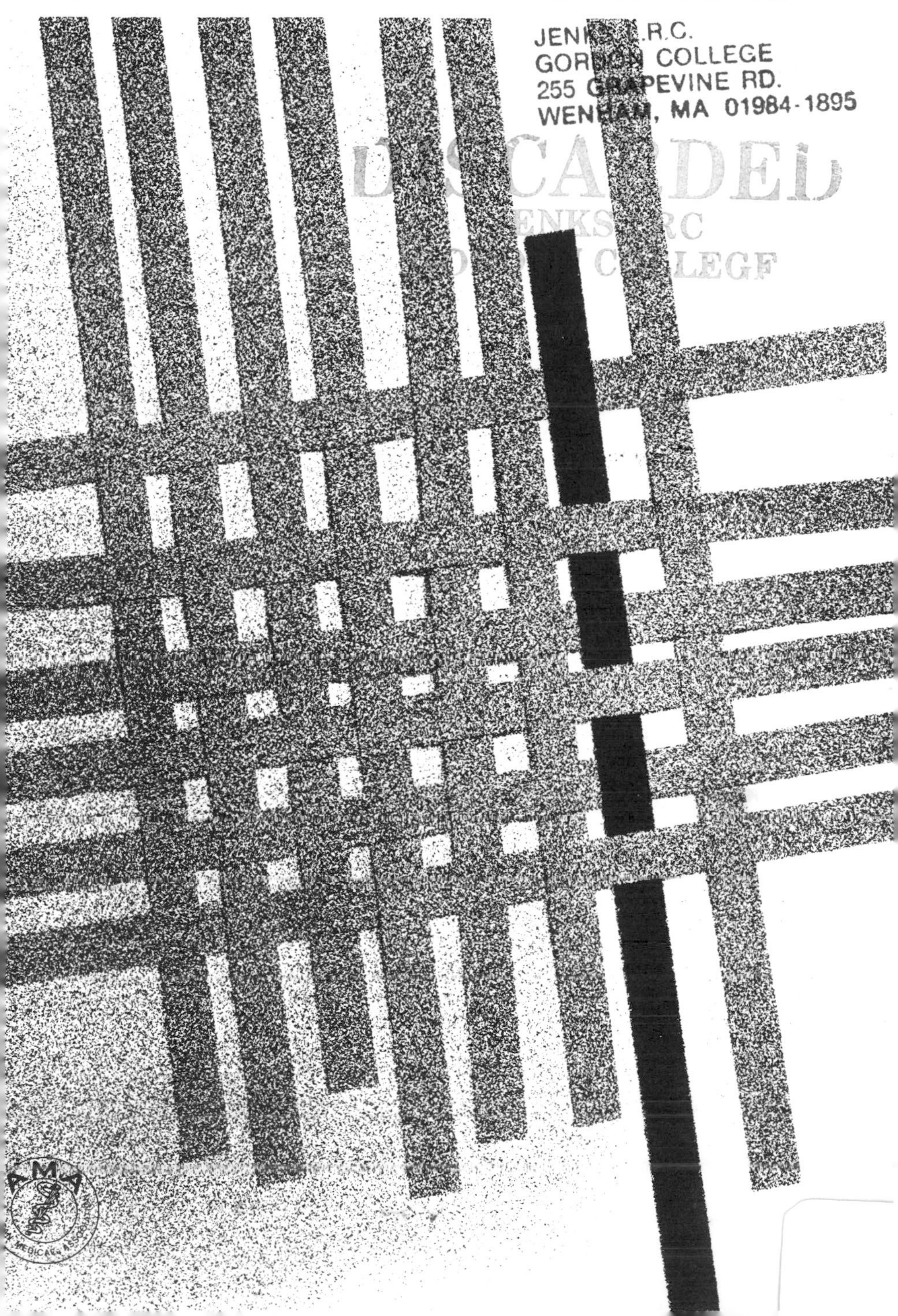

Library of Congress Catalogue Number 86-72784

ISBN: 0-89970-223-6

Additional copies can be ordered from:

Book & Pamphlet Fulfillment OP-314/6

P.O. Box 10946

Chicago, IL 60610

HEC:88-22:1M:2/88

AMA Handbook On Mental Retardation

Editors:

Herbert J. Grossman, M.D.
Professor
Departments of Pediatrics, Neurology,
and Psychiatry
University of Michigan Medical School
Ann Arbor, Michigan

George Tarjan, M.D.
Emeritus Professor of Psychiatry
U.C.L.A. School of Medicine
Los Angeles, California

Editorial Coordinator:

Valerie L. Vivian
Senior Research Associate
American Medical Association
Chicago, Illinois

Published by the American Medical Association
Division of Clinical Science
Chicago, Illinois

Printed in cooperation with Elwyn Institutes
Elwyn, Pennsylvania

child's environment — if begun early enough — may ameliorate a lifetime disability.

The physician plays a key role not only in diagnosis and treatment but in coordination of services for the mentally retarded patient. That role was emphasized in the AMA's Statement of Purpose at its April 1964 Conference on Mental Retardation: "The medical profession has a clearly defined responsibility in the early detection of retardation and in planning for and obtaining optimal care for the retarded."

To properly counsel, represent, and refer mentally retarded patients and their families, physicians — especially pediatricians, family physicians, internists, psychiatrists, and neurologists — should be familiar with the current definition of mental retardation; classification methods; diagnostic procedures; techniques for psychological assessment and patient management; special service needs; economic and legal considerations; and hopes for the future.

Improved methods of fetal and infant care now permit survival of many mentally retarded and other handicapped infants who once would have died at birth. Thus, the number of families who need guidance in managing mentally retarded children is greater than ever before. The physician also is likely to see more mentally retarded patients because of the current emphasis on retaining these persons in the community, where they can enjoy family life and community services.

A mentally retarded child presents unique problems that require individual solutions. That child occupies a place on a continuum of children who develop slowly or rapidly. The mentally retarded child, for example, may be only a step below a "normal" child diagnosed as a slow learner. By utilizing knowledge of the normal processes of growth and development and by imaginative application of skills and techniques employed with all children, a physician can effectively tailor services to the entire range of developing children.

Most previous publications on mental retardation have been child-oriented, but there is an increasing awareness that retarded youngsters become adults who have needs that must be addressed as well. Also receiving more attention are factors other than biological that play an important role in the lives of retarded individuals, such as family relationships, living arrangements, educational opportunities, community interaction, political priorities, legal rights, and prevocational and vocational training and employment. This book addresses these and other issues affecting mentally retarded persons of all ages.

The practicing physician faces a subtle and complex situation in dealing with a mentally retarded patient and that patient's family. Adherence to the basic tenets of good medical practice will enhance appropriate therapies. One such tenet is that management of problems of a multifactorial nature requires collaboration with allied disciplines and community agencies. Physicians also should encourage continued intensified research, as well as better preparation at the medical school and postgraduate levels. In so doing, physicians can improve the chances for present and future generations of mentally retarded individuals to lead healthy and happy lives.

Table of Contents

CHAPTER ONE

Historical Overview and Contemporary Concerns

The first distinction between mental illness and mental retardation was made in 1845. The initial classification system, based on language, separated persons with no speech from those who could say a few words and those who could speak in simple sentences. This one-dimensional system gave way to others as developments in medicine and pathology identified multiple causes of mental retardation.

In 1866, Langdon Down classified idiocy to provide optimal assistance in diagnosis, prognosis, and treatment. Down described three etiologic groups: congenital idiocy, developmental idiocy, and accidental injury. Eleven years later, a medical textbook listed 12 etiologic subdivisions of mental retardation. Still later, researchers agreed that two parallel groupings of the mentally retarded were useful: one from the point of view of educability and the other from a biological standpoint. During the 1970s, some classification systems offered both a behavioral category (based on severity of behavior deficit associated with impairment of IQ) and a biomedical category.

Developments in mental retardation over the past few decades have reflected the rapidly changing nature of the field. An example is the current practice of educating mentally retarded children within the public school system and keeping them in the mainstream of community life. As recently as the 1940s, few mentally retarded individuals received any special care at home. The traditional resource for "out-of-home" care was the large state-supported institution.

In the past, many state institutions and their program components had few individualized therapeutic goals and seldom attempted to evaluate treatment and management. Basic demographic and epidemiologic information was not available on newly admitted patients or on those in residence. The development, adjustment, or lack of adjustment of patients often went unmonitored. No estimate was made of the probability of a patient's acquiring daily living skills or the chance of his or her release from the institution. Discharges were few and turnover rates low.

Within that system, mentally retarded individuals appeared to fall into one of two major groups. Young children with severe retardation and physical handicaps constituted one group. Most institutions excluded these children from admission; when they were admitted, they received inadequate medical and nursing care and were likely to die early. The other group was composed of mildly retarded adolescents--many from underprivileged environments--who often entered institutions as a consequence of minor delinquency or because they had been excluded from local schools as a result of behavioral problems. For them, institutional care and educational resources also were inadequate.

After World War II, the health care system responded to the needs of retarded persons by adding new beds to existing institutions. However, additional beds did not eliminate waiting lists; enlargement of facilities only gave parents hope for somewhat earlier admission dates. Generally, children in institutions were kept idle. Some were restrained, and very few received consistent or constant care.

Thus, mentally retarded persons were housed "out of sight and out of mind." They also were well out of the social conscience. Public school programs for retarded children existed only in a few communities at the discretion of local school boards.

Significant advances in caring for mentally retarded persons began in the late 1950s and early 1960s, as general dissatisfaction with the level of institutional care mounted among health professionals and consumers. At that time, local and national efforts were made both to improve care in institutions and to develop alternatives to institutionalization.

In 1962, President Kennedy's Panel on Mental Retardation produced a blueprint for national action. His historic message to Congress on mental illness and mental retardation resulted in laws providing for construction and staffing of community facilities; university-based research, clinical, and teaching centers; training of special teachers; and expansion of services for the care of retarded persons, including the planning of comprehensive services in each state. Institutional programs were strengthened through demonstration projects and inservice training.

Other developments, although not directly focused on retardation, benefited the field. Examples are creation of the National Institute on Child Health and Human Development and the Head Start Program. Professional associations, as well as individuals who in the past might have shown little interest in the field, became involved.

Also in the 1960s, the Joseph P. Kennedy, Jr. Foundation changed its approach toward retardation from supporting a few direct service programs to establishing several university-based research centers. The Foundation's International Awards Program attracted scientific recognition to mental retardation as a promising field of study.

Community-based programs and newer, smaller residential facilities were developed during the later 1960s. In 1968, for the first time, the number of mentally retarded persons residing in public institutions declined. While this trend is ongoing, institutional services still fill a need as part of the continuum of care.

The care of mentally retarded patients has continued to change since the 1960s. The approach at that time emphasized special programs designed and operated specifically for those who were mentally retarded. Now the goal is to provide care in the least restrictive setting, which includes integrating mentally retarded persons into broader categories, such as children in general or residents of a particular geographic region.

As we learn more about providing care for mentally retarded persons, the quality and diversity of available services steadily improve. The current philosophy regarding treatment and education is dynamic, with several options for care. Settings range from the patient's own home to a variety of community residential facilities. Many special services are increasingly available, including day care and developmental centers, foster care, and public school education. As a result of The Education for All Handicapped Children Act of 1975 (Public Law 94-142), public education for physically and mentally handicapped children now is mandatory. In addition, there are numerous sheltered work settings and opportunities in competitive employment. Information on these and other social, economic, and legal developments is included in later chapters.

Among the major issues of concern regarding mentally retarded individuals today are the following:

1. *Socioeconomically disadvantaged individuals are overrepresented among the mildly retarded*, who constitute approximately 75% of the retarded population. Within that mildly retarded group, there are eight times as many youngsters from socioeconomically disadvantaged backgrounds as from middle class backgrounds.

2. *Evaluation of individuals in certain population groups by the use of traditional intelligence tests is questionable.* Safeguards have been enacted into federal and state law because of the belief that tests may be misused in the diagnosis of mental retardation and placement into treatment. These safeguards ensure that diagnosis and treatment do not rest on a single determinant, such as an IQ test or interview, but on a combination of test results, interviews with persons who are acquainted with the child, and observations of the child's behavior.

3. *Systematic data are lacking about what happens to mentally retarded individuals* after they are discharged from various settings. While it is possible to monitor retarded persons in public institutions, little is known about those who leave or, for that matter, those who do not even enter. Scant information is available about their way of life or level of adjustment in their communities. The closed system with potential for close accountability has given way to an open system in which accountability is less well measured. This shift from specialized to more general services makes it especially important to assure that retarded persons will not be forgotten when competing with others for services. One risk of "mainstreaming" is that the specific interests of the mentally retarded individual may not be given high priority in the general system of services.

Practical responses to contemporary concerns about mental retardation probably will come not from special programs for the mentally retarded but from advances in overall opportunities for education, employment, and health care.

CHAPTER TWO

Definitions and Classification

Since scientific and social strides in the field of mental retardation have been accompanied by changes in terminology, a basic understanding of currently accepted definitions and classification is important.

Currently Accepted Terms

Mental retardation. The term "mental retardation" refers to significantly subaverage general intellectual functioning that results in or is associated with impairments in adaptive behavior and is manifested during the developmental period.* Although many states, schools, and other entities define mental retardation differently, this definition is used increasingly among professionals and is consistent with that of the American Psychiatric Association (Diagnostic and Statistical Manual of Mental Disorders [DSM-III]) and that of the World Health Organization (International Classification of Diseases [ICD-9]).

General intellectual functioning. This term is operationally defined as the result of an assessment utilizing one or more individually administered standardized general intelligence tests developed for that purpose.

Significantly subaverage. The term "significantly subaverage" is defined as an IQ of 70 or lower on standardized measures of intelligence. The upper limit of 70 is intended only as a guideline; it can be extended to 75 or more, depending on the reliability of the intelligence test used. This is particularly true if behavior also is impaired and if that impairment is clinically determined to be the result of deficits in reasoning and judgment.

---

*Grossman HJ (ed): *Classification in Mental Retardation.* American Association on Mental Deficiency, 1983.

Impairments in adaptive behavior. Those that occur during the developmental period are defined as significant limitations in an individual's ability to meet the standards of maturation, learning, personal independence, and/or social responsibility expected of persons of the same age level and cultural group, as determined by clinical assessment and (usually) standardized scales.

Developmental period. This is the period between conception and the 18th birthday. Deficits in development may be manifested by slow, arrested, or incomplete development resulting from brain damage, degenerative processes in the central nervous system, or regression from previously normal states due to psychosocial factors.

Educable, trainable, totally dependent. In terms of educational potential, retarded children are sometimes described as "educable," "trainable," or "totally dependent." The educable individual may achieve academic competence at the fourth or fifth grade level, a moderate amount of social adjustment, and a satisfactory degree of self-support in occupations that do not require abstract thought. The trainable child may attain an acceptable level of self-care; social adjustment to home and neighborhood; and a degree of economic usefulness in the home, residential facility, or sheltered workshop. The totally dependent child requires assistance in personal care and usually permanent residential care outside the home.

Interface with Other Categories of Definition

The most important areas of interface are developmental disabilities, learning disabilities, autism, and attention deficit disorders.

Developmental disability. In the 1970s, the term "developmental disability" became popular largely because of wording in federal funding bills (Public Laws 94-103 and 95-602). As used in the Developmental Disabilities Assistance and Bill of Rights Act, the term refers to a severe, chronic disability "attributable to a mental or physical impairment or combination of mental and physical impairments that are manifested before age 22, are likely to continue indefinitely, and result in substantial functional limitations in three or more areas of major life activity."

Areas of functional limitation are most applicable to severe forms of mental retardation. For the severely retarded, defined areas of limitation include self-care, receptive and expressive language, learning, mobility, self-direction, capacity for independent living, and economic self-sufficiency. Mildly retarded individuals may have impairments in some areas of learning and self-direction but become self-sufficient in adulthood.

Children with other conditions (eg, cerebral palsy, autism, epilepsy) may be, but are not necessarily, developmentally disabled. Many individuals with those conditions function at retarded levels intellectually. In fact, mentally retarded persons constitute the majority of individuals in the categories covered by the definition of developmental disability.

Learning disability. Public Law 94-142 refers to a broad category of students who share the problem of difficulty in academic learning, especially reading and mathematics. The term "learning disability" refers to children who have a disorder in one or more of the basic psychological processes involved in understanding or using spoken or written language. Disabilities may be manifested in disorders of listening, thinking, talking, reading, writing, or math. They include conditions that have been described as perceptual handicaps, brain injury, minimal brain dysfunction, dyslexia, developmental aphasia, etc. They do not include learning problems that are due primarily to visual, hearing, or motor handicaps; mental retardation; emotional disturbances; or environmental disadvantages.

Mental retardation is not the only cause of diminished capacity to learn. A child who seems mentally retarded may suffer from defective hearing or vision, an emotional disorder, a perceptual handicap, a chronic illness, or chronic malnutrition. The physician's judgment is an important element in diagnosing retardation after these and other conditions have been ruled out.

Infantile autism. DSM-III defines infantile autism as a lack of responsiveness to other persons, impairment in communication skills, and bizarre responses to various stimuli in the environment--all developing within the first 30 months of life. Infantile autism may be associated with known organic conditions, such as maternal rubella or phenylketonuria. Approximately two-thirds of autistic children function in the mentally retarded range.

Attention deficit disorder. As defined in DSM-III, the essential features of attention deficit disorder are signs of developmentally inappropriate inattention and impulsiveness. Previously, several other terms were used to designate this disorder, including hyperkinetic reaction of childhood, hyperkinetic syndrome, hyperactive child syndrome, minimal brain damage, minimal brain dysfunction, minimal cerebral dysfunction, and minor cerebral dysfunction. The American Psychiatric Association states that "attention deficit" is an appropriate name for this disorder because attentional difficulties are prominent and virtually always present. Also, while excessive motor activity often diminishes in adolescence, difficulties in attention usually persist. Mental retardation may be found in combination with attention deficit disorder.

Two subtypes of the active disorder generally are recognized: attention deficit disorder with hyperactivity and attention deficit disorder without hyperactivity. However, it is not known conclusively whether these are two forms of a single disorder or two distinct disorders. Finally, a residual subtype has been designated for individuals once diagnosed as having attention deficit disorder with hyperactivity, in whom hyperactivity is no longer present but other signs of the disorder persist.

*Dual Diagnosis**

Dual diagnosis is a recently coined term that refers to persons diagnosed as both mentally retarded and mentally disturbed. Although viewed by some professionals as denoting a previously unidentified category of individuals, the term introduces nothing new that is helpful to patient or physician.

At one time in the past, two views of mental retardation and mental illness competed. One held that a retarded person's disturbed behavior was solely a learned reaction to environmental factors and did not represent a mental illness. The other claimed that a retarded individual's cognitive defect precluded the development of an emotional conflict sufficient to be considered a mental illness. Both views, although generated by opposing premises, agreed that not only could retarded persons not suffer from mental disorders but that they could not experience emotions common among nonretarded persons and that, in effect, they were not fully human.

As the popularity of these views waned and as clinical observations testified to the retarded person's vulnerability to mental illness, a new set of scientifically unsupported myths came into being, such as the belief that mental disorders in the retarded were of a different kind, usually "organic," and thus were untreatable.

The label "dual diagnosed," while perpetuating these myths, implies nothing specific: A "normal" individual who is bald and short-sighted is also dual diagnosed, since he suffers from both alopecia and myopia. When used to label a mentally retarded person, the term "dual diagnosis" implies that he or she suffers from a special illness.

---

*Adapted from Szymanski L and Grossman HJ: *Dual Implications of Dual Diagnosis*. May, 1984.

In recent years, as a result of modern clinical findings and experience, it has been recognized that retarded persons are indeed vulnerable to mental disorders, perhaps even more so than nonretarded individuals. It has further been recognized that mental disorders in retarded persons can be diagnosed by the same criteria and treated with the same approaches as mental disorders in nonretarded individuals. In accordance with the philosophy of normalization, it has been suggested that community mental health resources should have responsibility for providing mental health services to all, regardless of IQ. Efforts have been launched to include information and experience in mental retardation in the training curricula of mental health professionals, thus enabling them to integrate retarded persons into their patient load.

Classification

While mental retardation can be defined in terms of the individual's impairments in intellectual function and social adaptation, specific classification from an etiologic point of view is difficult because more than 250 causes of mental retardation have been identified. However, classification is necessary to provide objective data upon which to base legislation, funding, and program planning. The current classification system serves both policy-making and clinical functions.

Mentally retarded persons do not fall neatly into categories. Like other patients, they vary widely in degree of intellectual capacity and social adaptability. Some have associated physical handicaps and emotional problems; others do not. Some require protective care; others achieve a striking degree of independence.

While no distinct lines exist within the mentally retarded population, two subgroups can be identified for purposes of treatment. One is the "clinical type," which is found in about 25% of the retarded population. These individuals generally have a central nervous system disease, usually have IQs in the moderately retarded range or below, have associated handicaps and physical signs, and are typically diagnosed at birth or during early childhood. The remaining 75% comprise the other subgroup. These individuals seem to be neurologically intact; usually have no easily detectable physical signs or clinical laboratory evidence of retardation; have intelligence levels in the mildly retarded range; and are heavily concentrated in lower socioeconomic groups, which are characterized by low income, limited educational opportunities, unskilled occupations, and a generally impoverished environment. Their families must concentrate on meeting basic survival needs and usually lack the means or skills to provide their children with stimulating conversation, books, music, travel, and other intellectual and cultural advantages bestowed on many children of middle- and upper-income families.

Many children from less fortunate families attain school age unequipped with the experience or skills needed for formal learning. Some are deficient in the language and abstract thinking abilities required for reading, writing, and counting. Many of these children perform at the borderline level and become those who fill the special education classes. Their failure to learn is compounded by frustration and anxiety.

In some situations, biological and sociocultural influences interact within a child. Unfavorable conditions may modify normal progress so that functional retardation appears. In the child who is already handicapped by a biological disability, developmental progress may be further slowed by unfavorable experiential factors such as poverty, distorted patterns of parental care, or inappropriate institutionalization.

The 1983 classification system of the American Association on Mental Deficiency is consistent with that of the American Psychiatric Association and the World Health Organization and facilitates communication for diagnosis, treatment, and research (see Table 1).

Table 1
Level of Mental Retardation Indicated By IQ Range Obtained On Measures of General Intellectual Functioning*

Term	IQ range
Mild retardation	50-55 to approx. 70
Moderate retardation	35-40 to 50-55
Severe retardation	20-25 to 35-40
Profound retardation	Below 20-25

*Grossman HJ (ed): *Classification in Mental Retardation.* American Association on Mental Deficiency, 1983.

Criteria for classification. Classification according to the AAMD system generally is based on measured intelligence or intelligence quotient scores. (Some of the problems involved in this approach will be explored in Chapter IV.) To be categorized as mentally retarded according to the AAMD definition, however, an individual also must be deficient in adaptive behavior (social competence expected for one's chronologic age and culture). Generally, from childhood a mentally retarded person develops at a below-average rate and has difficulties in learning, social adjustment, and economic productivity. The nature of the impairment varies with the individual's age. In those younger than school age, it may be a lag in self-help, locomotion, eating, and communication skills. In school-aged children, it may be difficulty in learning. At an adult level, it may be inability to remain independent or to meet employment requirements. However, many mentally retarded individuals do become independent adults.

Mild, moderate, severe, and profound. By professional consensus, an upper IQ limit of approximately 70 is the commonly accepted guideline in classifying an individual as mentally retarded (see Table 1). A person with an IQ of 75 also may be considered mentally retarded if there are associated deficits in adaptive behavior. Most individuals with IQs of less than 70 require special services during the school years, because they are limited in their adaptive competence. Although persons with IQs over 70 also may need assistance at times, their needs are less compelling.

Before publication of the 1983 AAMD Manual on Classification, the upper IQ limit for identifying mental retardation was two standard deviations below the mean and was indicated in specific numbers. Now, the standard of "approximately 70" avoids the "numbers game" and allows flexibility in making clinical judgments. Such judgments include assessment of the individual's adaptive behavior and level of function, taking into account intellectual, affective, motivational, social, and motor abilities. Within the framework of the present classification system, an individual may meet the criteria at one time but not at another. As a result of alterations in intellectual functioning, adaptive behavior, or the expectations of society, he or she may be classified in different ways at different times.

Most individuals who are classified as "mildly" retarded differ from nonretarded persons only in their rate and degree of intellectual development. In many cases, their retardation is not apparent until they enter school. Many lose their identity as retarded individuals when, as adults, they enter the labor force and daily community life.

"Moderately" retarded persons usually show developmental delays before they reach school age. However, appropriate community-based education throughout their developmental years can prepare many of these individuals to live satisfying and productive lives. "Severely" and "profoundly" retarded persons show the most pronounced developmental problems and frequently have handicaps in addition to mental retardation.

Diagnosis of severe or profound retardation usually is made in infancy or early childhood. These children often have medically defined syndromes, and laboratory findings indicate organic involvement.

Judgment in Classifying Mentally Retarded Individuals

Medical diagnosis, psychological evaluation, and classification of retardation are closely intertwined. While classification is important in terms of epidemiology, medical diagnosis and psychological evaluation are more useful in assessing an individual's prognosis and quality of life.

The "rules" for classification of mental retardation are not hard and fast. At best, the classification system is only a guideline for diagnosis, treatment, and prognosis. The impersonality of the system does not permit analysis for discrepancies between measured intelligence and adaptive behavior, and in many cases it is not possible to categorize an individual. This is particularly true at the upper levels of mental retardation in a mildly retarded person.

CHAPTER THREE

Medical Diagnosis

The diagnosis of mental retardation involves much more than making decisions based on test scores. Physicians ideally employ a carefully balanced combination of techniques to identify biomedical causes and attendant psychosocial factors. Assessment is a dynamic process that must be tailored to the needs of each patient and is most meaningful when accomplished over a period of time.

Although diagnosis of mental retardation follows a pattern similar to that of other disorders, it is particularly challenging because the recognized protocols are constantly changing as understanding of the clinical and behavioral components increases. Nonetheless, the basics of history, physical examination, and carefully selected laboratory tests are involved. Within this framework, several factors are weighed. These may include identifiable biological syndromes, both medical and developmental history, neurologic examination, special tests (including biochemical and chromosomal studies), and behavioral evaluation.

Increasing emphasis is being placed on behavior, social adaptation, and developmental function in evaluating a potentially mentally retarded patient. Thus, the physician does not assess the patient in isolation but considers how well that patient interacts with his or her environment. The results of thorough medical and neurologic examinations and carefully selected laboratory tests are balanced with recommendations of other professionals and observations of the patient's family.

Importance of early diagnosis. Early identification of possible mental retardation is crucial to success in management. It affords the physician a long observation period in which to gather data, make a diagnosis, and develop an appropriate treatment plan. Detection and diagnosis of an underlying biological abnormality, for example, may lead to prevention of brain disease and subsequent retardation. Screening procedures in hospitals, clinics, and private practice can contribute to identification of certain high-risk patients for careful follow-up.

Early diagnosis is equally important for children who have been "environmentally deprived." Evidence suggests that exposure to a good preschool and other stimulating experiences may enhance the learning process as well as the social adjustment of such children, many of whom later become self-supporting and productive adults. Early identification also helps prevent situations in which parents--unaware of their child's limitations--make unrealistic demands, thereby aggravating the child's condition and further inhibiting development and function.

Diagnosis by Age and Severity

The physician is most likely to identify a moderately, severely, or profoundly retarded child in the office setting (or in the hospital nursery in the case of a newborn), while a mildly retarded child is more likely to be identified by a teacher or nurse in school and then referred to the physician for evaluation.

Moderate, severe, and profound retardation. Moderately, severely, or profoundly retarded persons represent 20% to 25% of the retarded population. Specific diagnoses include Down syndrome, cranial anomalies, genetic defects, and cerebral palsy as well as neurologic sequelae of other disorders (eg, traumas, infections, neurotropic poisons). Organic components (eg, musculoskeletal malformation, physical handicaps of ambulation and arm-hand use, sensory impairment) are common in these cases. Developmental milestones are grossly delayed in such children, and their behavior is consistent with their degree of mental impairment.

From birth to the end of the first year, diagnosis is less difficult in children with organic damage associated with developmental deficiency, such as that observed in Down syndrome, microcephaly, and hydrocephaly. Intellectual deficit in such children often is severe or profound (in some cases, an IQ of less than 35).

During the preschool years, previously undiagnosed conditions may become apparent through delays in walking, speech, and habit training or poor coordination. Presenting complaints may include simplicity of play, inability to form sentences, lack of imagination, and choice of playmates who are younger.

Mild retardation. Mildly retarded individuals (75% to 80% of the retarded population) are more difficult to diagnose, because they usually lack the physical handicaps and congenital malformations that characterize more severe degrees of retardation. In infancy, the mildly retarded child often is difficult or impossible to diagnose because of the broad range of variation in normal developmental patterns.

The mildly retarded child (IQ of 50-70) usually is first identified during the preschool and school years because of problems in academic performance, often accompanied by aggressive, withdrawn, or negative behavior. Multiple factors--biological and psychogenic--may interact to produce the retardation syndrome. Because these unfavorable factors often tend to cluster in underprivileged socioeconomic groups, the term "socio-culturally retarded" has been used to describe such children. After testing, mildly retarded patients often are referred for appropriate educational placement and later join the semi-skilled and unskilled labor force. Some even are able to secure professional and managerial positions. Many become relatively well adjusted and lose their identity as mildly retarded individuals.

Diagnosis by Biological Syndrome

Certain biological syndromes may be related to mental retardation, although their presence is not invariably pathogenic. Two basic types of clinical clues are specific morphologic or anatomical signs and progressive developmental deterioration.

The list of known metabolic disorders and progressive disorders of central processes associated with mental retardation is extensive (see Table 2). Although there is a growing appreciation of these syndromes, as a group they are relatively rare.

Laboratory and imaging studies should be used selectively in these disorders. CAT scans may be appropriate in some cases but not in others. Chromosomal studies may not be necessary for most mentally retarded children but should be considered if a patient has multiple anomalies--especially those affecting the face, ears, and distal extremities--or is born small for gestational age. Other indicators may include a maternal history of repeated spontaneous abortion, dermatoglyphic abnormalities, unusual facies, macro-orchidism, or a clinically recognizable genetic syndrome. Lysosomal storage diseases are suggested by regression or deterioration of motor and intellectual development, hepatosplenomegaly, skeletal dysostosis, cloudy cornea, cherry red macula, retinal degeneration, or observation of these symptoms in siblings. An inborn error in amino acid metabolism may be suggested by positive screening tests, unusual odors, metabolic acidosis, failure to thrive, lethargy, vomiting, unusual hair, ataxia, seizures, and other neurologic symptoms.

Developmental History and Assessment

A good psychological history and physical examination are basic diagnostic tools in cases of mental retardation. Elements of particular significance in planning a management program are a complete medical and developmental history, an assessment of the individual's interaction with his or her family, and an understanding of how the family views the patient. These aspects should be considered carefully to identify children who are at risk for developmental problems and those who need more extensive developmental assessment, to detect definitive patterns of developmental delay, and to identify factors that facilitate

Table 2
Identifiable Biochemical Disorders Affecting Amino Acids Associated With Mental Retardation[1]

Disease	Biochemical Characteristics	Clinical Features
Phenylketonuria (PKU) (Incidence: 1:10,000)	Increased plasma phenylalanine; phenylalanine metabolites in the urine. Some variants affect biopterin metabolism.	Delayed development, autism, seizures. These respond to a low phenylalanine diet. Variants require tetrahydrobiopterin supplementation.
Homocystinuria (Incidence: 1:150,000)	Plasma methionine often but not always increased; homocystine in urine. Several variants may affect folic acid/B_{12} metabolism.	Delayed development, bony overgrowth, dislocated lenses, thromboembolic strokes. Some forms respond to B_6 supplementation.
Maple Syrup Urine Disease (MSUD or branched chain ketoaciduria-BCK) (Incidence: 1:250,000)	Metabolic disturbance of leucine, isoleucine, valine. Branched chain amino acids are increased in blood and urine along with respective ketoacids in urine.	Seizures, delayed development, maple syrup odor. Variants: intermittent ataxia/altered alertness.
Urea cycle disorders (Incidence: 1:30,000?)	Variable hyperammonemia affecting all ages	Hyperammonemia also may occur in several organic acidurias.
(1) Carbamylphosphate synthetase I (C-P-S_1)	Without orotic aciduria	
(2) Ornithine transcarbamylase (OTC)	With orotic aciduria; sex-linked dominant	Vomiting, lethargy, seizures, coma (acute and/or chronic symptoms)
(3) Argininosuccinate synthetase (AS)	Citrullinemia	

Table 2 (Cont.)

Disease	Biochemical Characteristics	Clinical Features
(4) Argininosuccinate lyase (AL)	Argininosuccinic aciduria	Beaded scalp hair; delayed development
(5) Arginase (ARG)	Argininemia	Unique spastic diplegia and ataxia[2]
Other less common disorders of amino acids with mental retardation[3]		
(1) Histidinemia (Incidence: 1:18,000)	Increased plasma and urine histidine	Speech disorder; seizures, often benign
(2) Lysinemia (Incidence: 1:300,000)	Increased plasma and urine lysine	Delayed development
(3) Nonketotic glycinemia (NKG)[4] (Incidence: 1:150,000)	Increased plasma and urine glycine	Neonatal hypotonia, developmental delay in all ages

[1]Prepared by Richard Allen, MD, Professor of Pediatrics and Neurology, University of Michigan Medical School, 1983.

[2]Cerebral palsy and developmental delay may be associated with argininemia, a urea cycle disorder, and in the sex-linked Lesch-Nyham Syndrome (a disorder of purine metabolism associated with increased uric acid in the urine and absent hypoxanthine-guanine-phosphoribosyl transferase [GHPRT] measurable in red blood cells). This disorder is recognized clinically with athetoid cerebral palsy and self-mutilation (finger and lip chewing). Also, glutamic aciduria (Type I), with symptoms similar to those of cerebral palsy but without mutilation, is commonly associated with chronic metabolic acidosis.

[3]Some disorders with the variable association of neurological symptoms have specific amino acidurias without amino acidemia (elevated plasma levels) and include, specifically, Hartnup Disease and cystinuria. Presumably, a renal transport defect accounts for the amino aciduria.

[4]NKG should be differentiated from the several disorders known as the organic acidurias. These are associated with ketoacidosis, hyperammonemia, methylmalonic aciduria/propionic ccidemia, and hyperglycinemia and may be due to several different catabolic enzymes important in amino acid metabolism.
In some organic acidemias, the enzymes are responsive to vitamin (B_{12}, biotin) supplementation therapeutically.

(or inhibit) normal development (see Table 3). Finally, assessment procedures can delineate problems that are clearly amenable to corrective action.

Individual differences. The rate of physical development in children varies widely, and the dividing line between normal and pathologic development (as in growth or nutrition) can be indistinct. In borderline cases, the physician may need to perform serial examinations over several months to determine whether future growth processes may correct a perceived deviation.

Children also differ markedly in intellectual, psychological, social, and behavioral development. Normal age-level ranges are extremely wide, and the determination of developmental progress is always multifactorial. Concepts of "normal" are vaguely defined by a constantly changing social culture rather than by objective statistical averages. Therefore, the sequence of development is more important in assessing a child's need for professional help than a developmental timetable based on age-linked averages.

If "growth process" is a standard of normality, the physician will consider whether a child's maturation is progressing at a reasonable rate. However, even "reasonable rate" is a matter of clinical judgment.

Slowed, arrested, or regressing development in the child may indicate an identifiable problem. However, no aspect of development--whether physiological, psychological, intellectual, or social--proceeds in a completely linear manner. Instead, each facet usually is marked by several spurts, plateaus, and regressions. If these arrests and regressions are temporary and resolve themselves, they do not require treatment. If, however, the child remains fixed at an immature level, or if regression continues unabated, professional intervention may be required to prevent one type of developmental arrest from interfering with the totality of physical and mental growth processes.

Table 3
Sample "Screening" Questions for Various Developmental Levels From Pregnancy To 8 Years of Age*

Examples of Questions	Illustrations of "At Risk" Responses
(A) PREGNANCY	
1. How often do you visit with your parents or other family?	1. Rarely.
2. Has anything happened either before or during your pregnancy that causes you to worry about the baby?	2. My husband calls his ex-wife all the time. It upsets me terribly. I'm afraid it will hurt the baby.
3. Do you have any condition that you think might be made worse by being pregnant?	3. Yes. I had a kidney infection last year.
4. What was your reaction when you felt life?	4. I don't remember.
5. Is your husband (the father of the child) much help?	5. He's like another child to take care of.
6. How would you compare the way you feel now with the way you normally feel?	6. Everything hurts. I can't get my housework done. I never sleep now.
(B) NEONATAL PERIOD (up to 4 weeks)	
1. Do you think you can tell your baby's cry from others?	1. No. They all sound the same to me.
2. How does the baby compare with what you imagined he/she would be like when you were pregnant?	2. Very different. He's too active. He never gives me any peace. And he doesn't look like either of us. I wonder if he's really mine.
3. As far as you know, is everything OK with the baby?	3. The doctor told me he was fine. But my girlfriend lost her baby when he was 4 months old. Maybe something will happen.
4. Are you getting any help with the baby?	4. I'd rather not. I really don't trust anyone else with him.
5. How has your husband (mate) reacted to the baby?	5. I think he's pretty jealous of him.
6. Are you satisfied with your ability to take care of the baby?	6. He's really a mystery to me. I never know what he wants. He keeps me running in circles.

*Developed by Richard L. Cohen, MD, University of Pittsburgh, Western Psychiatric Institute and Clinic, School of Medicine, Department of Psychiatry, Division of Child Psychiatry.

Table 3 (Cont.)

Examples of Questions	Illustrations of "At Risk" Responses
(C) LATER INFANCY (up to 15 or 18 months)	
1. Does the baby seem to know you? How can you tell? (about 4 months)	1. I'm not sure. He smiles at me, but he smiles at everyone the same way.
2. What does the baby seem to be interested in? (about 8 months)	2. He's pretty quiet. He mostly likes to look at the TV.
3. What does he do when a stranger comes into the room? (about 8 months)	3. Anyone can pick him up. He really doesn't seem to favor anybody.
4. Does the baby like to explore things? (about 1 year)	4. Yes, but I'm afraid he'll hurt himself. I put most things out of his reach, and I always keep him in the kitchen or his own room.
5. Does he try to get your attention in other ways than crying? Does he try to do things with you?	5. No, not very often.
6. Has he become fairly regular in his habits of eating, sleeping, elimination, etc.?	6. No. It depends entirely on his mood, or maybe mine. I never know what the day will be like.
(D) TODDLERHOOD	
1. What kinds of toys does he seem to like to play with?	1. Well, he really doesn't have any of his own. He plays with his six-year-old brother's toys.
2. When he wants something, will he try to ask for it?	2. No. He points or cries.
3. What kinds of things can he do for himself? For instance, how well can he feed himself?	3. Oh, I don't think kids can be expected to do much at this age. Besides, he makes such a mess. It's easier for me to do it.
4. Does he seem to say "no" a lot? How do you handle that?	4. I just can't seem to please him. Everything I do is wrong. Maybe he'll go through the rest of his life rebelling against everything.
5. How does he act when other children his age are around?	5. He usually ignores them completely.
6. How does he act when you and your husband go out for the evening?	6. He makes a real fuss. The sitter says it takes hours for him to quiet down. I guess I'm thinking about him the whole time we're out.

Table 3 (Cont.)

Examples of Questions	Illustrations of "At Risk" Responses
(E) PRESCHOOL YEARS	
1. What kinds of things do you still have to do for him?	1. He comes to me for almost everything. He still wants me or my husband to go to the bathroom with him.
2. How does he act with children his own age?	2. He can't share. He always has to be the boss or he won't play.
3. Does he (she) like to imitate his father (her mother)?	3. No. I can't think of any examples of that.
4. Does he sleep through the night for the most part?	4. No. He gets up a lot. He seems to have nightmares. Or he will wet the bed and then want to sleep with us.
5. Is he showing interest in his own body — and in his parents' and siblings'?	5. Mostly, he's afraid of getting hurt. If he falls or cuts himself, he cries a lot and asks a lot of questions about whether he will get well again.
6. What is he interested in? Does he ask lots of questions or want you to read stories to him?	6. He still likes to play with his baby toys. He avoids new things or new ideas. He really wants things to stay the same.
(F) 6 TO 8 YEAR PERIOD	
1. How has he taken to the idea of going to school every day?	1. He complains and fusses a lot. He's full of excuses. We have to stay on top of him the whole time.
2. Does he like to play games with other children?	2. Yes, but they don't last very long. He likes to change the rules if he's losing, and they get angry at him.
3. What does he talk about being when he grows up?	3. We never hear him talk about anything like that. I think he has the idea that he's going to stay with us forever.
4. What is he like when he gets sick?	4. You've never seen a bigger baby. He acts like a two-year-old.
5. How does he act toward the new baby?	5. He's very jealous. We have to watch him all the time to make sure he doesn't hurt the baby.
6. How does he react to doing chores around the house?	6. We've stopped that. We have to nag so much, it's easier for us to do it.

Human relationships. An infant's relationship with the mother is both biological and social. In infancy, social and emotional needs are met in close association with the mother's response to the child's bodily needs, whereas in early childhood, the influences of society and culture are mediated primarily through nurturing adults and are gradually augmented through the child's relationships with other significant persons. Through this process, a child acquires character, as well as the following attributes: curiosity and eagerness; a tendency to trust or mistrust; self-esteem or self-doubt; a capacity to solve problems through physical, intellectual, or social activity; an ability to cope with stress or defend against danger; a capacity for self-direction and self-control; and the ability to give and accept love.

Learning to discriminate between things and persons and becoming aware of oneself as a person distinct from others depend on the quality of the child's relationships. While adults may deliberately teach some attitudes, most of the child's perceptions and skills seem to be acquired through the daily experience of living in close relationship with emotionally significant persons.

Neither normal nor deviant development can be explained without understanding the nature, frequency, and intensity of the child's experiences with others. Therefore, the physician should consider the psychosocial aspects of family interaction. Evidence of environmental, social, or economic deprivation or lack of appropriate stimulation should be analyzed carefully. Good nurturing means care, concern, and training of the child. Development proceeds most favorably when comfort, loving care, and supportive experiences predominate over experiences that are painful, tension-producing, or psychologically frustrating. Deficits in nurturing may arise when caretakers are confused, rejecting, or highly ambivalent. Deficits also may be caused by events such as traumatic separations from emotionally important persons, discontinuity of care, deprivation, or physical abuse.

Certain problems cut across cultural and socioeconomic lines. For example, children often are brought to physicians because they are "bothering" someone in the family, school, or community. Deviations from normal in these cases usually are manifested by behavior that is socially unacceptable.

Some adverse experiences in the child's surroundings may be difficult to identify. For example, a lonely, depressed young mother who appears to be comfortable in the company of adults may be psychologically or physically unavailable to her child when the two are alone. Articulate and intelligent parents may mask their difficulties in nurturing their children. In these instances, clues usually come from the child's deviant development or symptomatic behavior rather than from what the parents report. Each case should be evaluated on the basis of how significant persons, especially the parents, have supported or impeded the child's development and have alleviated or heightened his or her problems.

Family assessment. Two aspects of family life should be considered: the family's perception of difficulties in the patient and other family members, and the adequacy of family interaction. Compared with siblings or peers, parents, grandparents, and other family members often can give valuable information about the child's development. They also may be helpful by recollecting delays in reaching usual norms in habit training and coordination, as well as delays in comprehension or use of language. (Inasmuch as quality and quantity of vocabulary are highly correlated with individual intelligence, an underdeveloped comprehension and speaking vocabulary may be a good clue to possible retardation in a child who sees and hears normally.)

The strengths of families also should be assessed. Employing such strengths can maximize the impact of services that are designed to support and mobilize the family for the child's benefit. Parental involvement in all aspects of assessment and programming has a direct bearing on whether the child will achieve lasting developmental gains.

Dangers of labeling. Physicians should be alert to the adverse effects of "labeling" children. Too often, a label will determine the kind of expectations that parents, teachers, and others have for a child. These expectations, in turn, shape their interactions with the child in such a way that his or her behavior becomes consistent with the label, thus making the label a self-fulfilling prophecy.

Developmental delay in early childhood does not necessarily warrant the label "mentally retarded." Such a label is justified only when there is a firm diagnosis based on known etiology, when the developmental outcome is relatively fixed, and when "labeling" is necessary for

Table 4
Child Development, Parent Development, and Family Developmental*

Child's Developmental Stages	Individual Developmental Tasks (Erickson)	Parent Development (Friedman)	Family Development (Solomon)
			The marriage
Infant	Trust	Learning the cues	Birth of the first child and subsequent childbearing
Toddler	Autonomy	Learning to accept growth and development	Redefinition of roles with the birth of each child
Preschool	Initiative	Learning to separate	Individuation of family members
School age	Industry	Learning to accept rejection, without deserting (permitting independence)	
Adolescence	Identity Intimacy	Learning to build a new life	Actual departure of the child Integration of loss

*Based on Prugh's delineation of concepts developed by E. H. Erickson (Childhood and Society, W. W. Norton & Company, New York, 1950); A. S. and D. B. Friedman (Parenting: A developmental process, *Pediatric Annals* 6:9, 1977); and M. A. Solomon (A developmental conceptual premise for family therapy, *Family Process* 12:179, 1973).

parental understanding. In all other instances, objective statements about the child's observed development and behavior, as well as his or her service needs, should suffice when discussing the child's condition with parents.

Appraising development. Assessing child development includes observation by the physician, parents, and others and the use of standardized tests. An understanding of normal development is useful in the diagnosis of mental retardation. Normal children reach certain predictable developmental milestones; assessment of progress in attaining those milestones should be an integral part of every well-baby examination. In developmental evaluation, the physician may find a simple assessment form helpful (see Table 4).

Although the child's development can be determined somewhat by direct examinations and tests, the physician can obtain much useful information from parents and other caregivers. Careful note should be made of items most likely to be remembered by parents, such as:

Child sits with support from 6 to 8 months
Sits alone from 8 to 10 months
Walks from 12 to 18 months
Talks from 18 to 24 months
Rides a tricycle at 3 years
Copies a square at 4 years

Additionally, toilet training is an important issue in child development, although progress in this area is strongly influenced by sociocultural factors.

Standardized assessment scales. While differences of opinion exist concerning the usefulness of standardized assessment scales in predicting the course of development of any child, these scales can be important in providing objective and measurable estimates of current behavioral functioning.

Table 5
Variables in Language Acquisition and Use*

Variables Affecting Language Acquisition and Use	Comprehension (Reception)	Production (Expression)	Pragmatics (Use of Language for Communication)
NEUROPSYCHOLOGICAL FACTORS			
1. Cognitive development	1. Delayed onset — slow development	1. Delayed onset — slow development	1. Delayed onset — slow development
2. Sensory: Auditory, Visual } Acuity and Perception	2. Does not develop (severe) to delayed onset (minimal) — auditory	2. Sound production diminishes at 6 mos. (auditory); delayed onset (visual)	2. Motor and motor + vocal (auditory)
3. (Speech) Motor Control	3. Not affected	3. Intelligibility of speech poor to fair (dysarthria); delayed onset (respiratory control)	3. Not affected
4. Attending, relating, motivation	4. Does not develop to delayed onset, depending on severity	4. Delayed onset or failure to develop; dysfluency (stuttering and cluttering)	4. Disordered or nonexistent
STRUCTURAL AND PHYSIOLOGICAL FACTORS			
1. Sensory: Auditory, Visual } End Organ Dysfunction	1. Delayed onset (minimal to moderate); poor to fair intelligibility (auditory)	1. Delayed onset — auditory	1. Motor and motor + vocal expression delayed onset (visual) — minimal
2. Cranial facial anomalies	2. Not affected	2. Intelligibility of speech related to structures affected and severity	2. Not affected
3. Laryngeal anomalies	3. Not affected	3. Limited voicing, including intensity, frequency, and quality disorders	3. Motor and motor + vocal expression — severe

*Table reproduced courtesy of David E. Yoder and Jon F. Miller, *Variables in Language Acquisition and Use,* unpublished paper, 1978.

Table 5 (Cont.)

Variables Affecting Language Acquisition and Use	Comprehension (Reception)	Production (Expression)	Pragmatics (Use of Language for Communication)
ENVIRONMENTAL FACTORS			
1. Social and cultural SES Language and dialect	1. Delayed onset (bilingual home)	1. Delayed onset, dialect reflective of culture and community	1. Not affected
2. Physical Experience Linguistic input (living situation)	2. Delayed onset	2. Delayed onset	2. Delayed onset, few communication needs

The physician should be concerned primarily with the child's present developmental status. If the infant is slow to cry or respond at a minimal level; to reach or grasp; or to sit, walk, or talk, more intensive study or consultation is warranted. Behavior observed should be noted on the chart so that the child's current performance can be compared with later abilities. Such records, kept consistently, enhance the physician's ability to identify not only the retarded child but also the child who might profit from a wide variety of immediate remedial procedures.

Most normal children vocalize a simple word or two meaningfully between 9 and 12 months and speak in two- or three-word sentences by 2 years. By 7 to 9 years, children usually overcome earlier errors of fluency and articulation. While significant deviations from these norms provide valuable clues to possible mental deficits, they do not in themselves indicate mental retardation (see Table 5).

Medical History

In addition to performing a thorough physical examination, the physician should obtain records of the child's birth, past medical and surgical care, and previous hospitalizations. Untoward episodes in the life of the child should be recorded. These might involve infections, accidents, seizures, unexplained crying bouts, apneic and cyanotic episodes, stiffness and limpness, behavioral disturbances, and progressive developmental or neurologic deterioration. Exploring certain aspects of familial or parental health status, such as relevant genetic information, blood group incompatibilities, fertility history of the mother, and her experiences in this pregnancy (including the history of labor and delivery), also can be helpful.

History at birth may suggest certain types of disorders. For example, low birth weight in a term neonate may indicate a dysmaturity syndrome or intrauterine growth retardation, both of which are associated with a significant incidence of neurologic difficulties.

Physical Examination

General body proportions. Shortened extremities suggest chondrodystrophy. Body asymmetry associated with short stature, occasionally accompanied by syndactyly, may suggest Silver syndrome (in which mental retardation usually is not present).

Head. Careful examination of the head can provide clues, if not specific diagnoses, to many problems. Some disorders are associated with a small head. For example, a very small head may indicate microcephaly, which may be familial or secondary to anoxia or damage due to intrauterine infections.

Increased biparietal diameter of the head may be seen in chronic subdural hematoma. Many of these problems are related to physical abuse and usually are accompanied by other evidence of physical trauma. Radiographic examination of the skull may reveal fractures.

A large head may indicate hydrocephalus, cerebral gigantism, generalized gangliosidosis, Hunter disease, Hurler disease, Tay-Sachs disease, or achondroplasia. Doll-like facies is characteristic of Tay-Sachs disease.

Tongue. A large tongue may be seen in cretinism, Down syndrome, hypoglycemia, Trisomy 17-18, Hurler disease, Hunter disease, generalized gangliosidosis, and Sanfilippo syndrome. Furrowed tongue occurs in Down syndrome, while lobulated tongue is seen in oral-facial-digital (OFD) syndrome.

Hair. Sparse, coarse, kinky hair (Menkes syndrome) that is devoid of pigmentation may suggest neurodegenerative disease, while monilethrix (brittle hair with shafts of varying diameters) often is associated with seizures, spasticity, and progressive clinical deterioration. In cretinism, the hair is coarse, brittle, and scanty, with the hairline far down on the forehead.

Confluence of the eyebrows and hypertrichosis is found in de Lange syndrome.

A white forelock suggests the presence of Waardenburg syndrome. Mental retardation usually is not present but may be considered because of unrecognized nerve deafness.

The appearance of a low V-shaped frontal hairline may suggest the median cleft face syndrome, in which there is an associated median cleft palate.

Eyes. Confluent eyebrows are characteristics of de Lange syndrome. Hypertelorism is seen in many variations from normal to abnormal. Congenital cataracts suggest Hallerman-Streiff syndrome, rubella, or oculo-cerebral-renal syndromes. Slant eyes are seen in Down syndrome, de Lange syndrome, cerebral gigantism, and Apert syndrome, among many others. Coloboma of the pupil may be seen in oculo-articulo-vertebral dysplasia, Trisomy 17-18, and several other disorders.

Ears. Abnormalities of the ears are present in many disorders; for example, very prominent antihelix suggests Down syndrome, while preauricular appendages and atresia of the external meatus occur in oculo-auricular-vertebral dysplasia.

Low-set ears are seen in the following syndromes and other disorders: Apert, Crouzon, Hallerman-Streiff, Pierre-Robin, Trisomy 13-15 and 17-18, Rubinstein-Taybi, and cri-du-chat.

Extremities. Syndactyly of fingers and toes suggests Apert syndrome, while broad thumbs and toes are seen in Rubinstein-Taybi syndrome. Tapered fingers may be seen in new dominant syndrome. Polydactyly suggests Laurence-Moon-Biedl syndrome, while syndactyly of toes and overlapping toes are associated with Ring chromosome 18.

Fifth finger overlapping the fourth, polydactyly, syndactyly, retroflexed thumbs, and "rocker bottom" feet are seen in Trisomy 13-15. Flexion of the hand with the index finger overlapping the third finger, "rocker bottom" feet, and short sternum are seen in Trisomy 17-18. Polydactyly or the syndactyly associated with cryptorchidism and/or hypospadias suggests the Smith-Lemli-Opitz syndrome.

Skin. Acrocyanosis may be seen in the Marinesco-Sjogren syndrome (mental retardation associated with cerebellar ataxia, bilateral cataracts, and short stature).

Adenoma sebaceum, with characteristic butterfly distribution over nose and cheeks, is seen in tuberous sclerosis. Other symptoms of this disorder include fibromas of the gums, nails, forehead, and scalp; cafe-au-lait spots; depigmentation and "orange peel" appearance of skin on the trunk, with generalized decreased pigmentation and hemangiomas; and graying hair.

Port-wine hemangioma, usually over one side of the face and forehead, suggests Sturge-Weber syndrome. Telangiectasia of the skin of the ears and conjunctiva of the eyes suggests ataxia-telangiectasia (Louis-Bar) syndrome. Blotching of the skin may be seen in familial dysautonomia. Ichthyosis may be seen in chondrodystrophica calcificans congenita and Sjogren-Larsson syndrome. Cafe-au-lait spots may be seen in neurofibromatosis, tuberous sclerosis, and ataxia-telangiectasia.

Neurologic Examination

Neurologic evaluation in the diagnosis of the mentally retarded child requires careful assessment of nervous system function as well as a complete physical examination. General observation may provide important clues that relate to the specific neurologic deficit.

The neurologic examination helps the physician determine the nature and location of a functional disturbance of the nervous system. A complete examination requires not only competence on the part of the examiner but the patient's ability to cooperate. With young infants and children, as well as patients who are unable to cooperate, professional observation becomes the most critical part of the examination. Several techniques that are not necessarily familiar or orthodox when applied to older, more cooperative individuals must be used.

One of the most critical facets in the neurologic examination of infants and young children is the assessment of their overall development, including mental status. The patient's general level of activity, cooperation, social responsiveness, and awareness of the situation are reviewed. Many tasks are evaluated with regard to expectations for a given age. Because certain abilities to function increase with chronologic age, and what may be perfectly normal at one age is considered abnormal at another, *developmental* neurology is most critical in the assessment of children.

Soft neurologic signs. Deficits may include gross and fine motor awkwardness (including gait, hopping, etc.), poor handwriting, minimal choreoathetoid movements, subtle asymmetry of deep tendon reflexes, asymmetrical clonus, right-left disorientation (ie, inability or difficulty in differentiating right from left), and isolated extensor toe sign not associated with other findings.

These findings may or may not be significant and, in themselves, do not specifically indicate a clinical syndrome. However, they are most likely to be observed in more severly mentally retarded individuals.

The physician uses diverse methods to evaluate soft neurologic signs in an attempt to systematically interpret the structure and function of the nervous system. Following an overall assessment of development, including handedness, the physician can assess the function of more clearly defined areas. For example, examination of the cranial nerves yields information about vision, hearing, smell, and taste; eye movements; pupillary function; sensation about the face and head; muscles of mastication; muscles of facial expression; equilibrium;

Table 6
Characteristic Signals For Concern

Age of Child	"Red Flags"	Questions for Parents	Interventions
0 to 3 months			
Vision	Does not lift head from prone position by 3 months of age Does not follow light brought into field of vision peripherally Does not engage in visual-social contact with mother Does not attend to new objects brought into view	History regarding visual problems in family such as: myopia glaucoma cataracts retinoblastoma Further questions related to mother's continued observation of child's visual interactions in family social situation	If any of these "red flags" are present, referral should be made immediately to an ophthalmologist.
Hearing	Does not startle at loud sounds Does not indicate auditory awareness by gross head movements or modification of behavior when talked to in normal tone of voice Does not respond to soft bell tone (Usual tuning fork is pitched too low to detect most hearing loss.)	Is child responsive to: parental/family vocalizations? household noises? accidental noises?	If any of these "red flags" are present, referral should be made to an audiologist who can perform tests such as: Brain Stem Evoked Response (BSER), audiometry, and other range sound audiometric evaluation.
Communication	Child does not relate to environment by visual gazing Child does not react to new environment (physician's office) Child does not have differentiated cry response Child does not engage in vocal play Nonresponsive or irritable infant Indications of maternal depression; difficulties with relationship	Questions relating to: infant's responsiveness to visual stimuli and interactions with family members upon their appearance Vocalizations Responsiveness to auditory/visual stimuli in normal home setting Feeling of mother toward child: Does mother enjoy child? Is she playful? Is infant playful? Is child responsive to mother? Are there family problems that make it difficult to interact with the child?	Referral for same diagnostic procedures as for visual/auditory impairment After evaluation, intervention strategy might be infant stimulation program

Table 6 (Cont.)

Age of Child	"Red Flags"	Questions for Parents	Interventions
3 to 6 months			
Vision	Indications of intercranial pressure (constantly crying infant) Infant does not attend to visual stimuli during physical examination Overly quiet child (may be compensating for visual impairment with auditory attentiveness) Does not reach out for mother or object until they are directly in front Does not reach out to strangers within his/her field of vision "Red Flags" noted for 0 to 3 months	Does infant respond to mother's presence by reaching? Does mother note infant's quietness and attentiveness/ responsiveness to sounds? Does child follow movements of mobile hung in front rather than directly above him/her?	Refer to ophthalmologist
Hearing	Does not show beginning localization of sound that increases from 3 to 6 months Does not respond to unfamiliar noises	Does baby turn his/her head in direction of household noises? Is baby intrigued by unfamiliar noises?	Referral as for previous age groups
Communication	Vocalization not present No progressive vocal imitation Does not quiet at sound of mother's voice Does not turn head/eyes in direction of sound	Does mother hear baby vocalize when she is not there? Are baby's sounds imitating mother's? Does baby engage in visual and auditory games?	As before, the issue is consideration of any special conditions and careful evaluation by specialist Mother/infant may respond to infant stimulation program
6 to 12 months			
Vision	Unusual use of mouth/ tongue to explore objects/ environment Some delay in motor development, especially related to postural changes (sitting, crawling) Attention span to given stimuli unusually long Cataracts, amblyopia "Red Flags" noted for 0 to 3, 3 to 6 months	Any unusual uses of mouth/tongue for exploration? Does child pay greater attention to voice cues and other sounds than to visual cues? Does child show unusual discomfort or crying (may be indications of intercranial pressure)? Does child use toys to make loud noises repetitively?	Refer to ophthalmologist Immediate referral to ophthalmologist Surgery during first year of life critical for future development

Table 6 (Cont.)

Age of Child	"Red Flags"	Questions for Parents	Interventions
Hearing	No indication of linguistic comprehension (does not respond to labels of "Mommy," "Daddy," "cookie")	Does child appear to understand simple questions (eg, "Where is Mommy?")?	Audiological examination
	Little imitation of vocalizations and speech patterns Marked reduction of vocalization No single words by 12 months	Does child imitate voice patterns? Is child trying to say single words? Are child's babbling vocalizations dropping off?	After evaluation, intervention strategy might be early amplification and parent/child total communication program
Communication	No word approximations No increased vocalization No signs of comprehension of simple questions (by 12 months) No increased imitation of vocalizations, intonations	Does child want to look at books with parents and identify pictures (by 12 months)? How much time can mother spend with child? Is child more fun to be with now? Do mother/child enjoy verbal games?	Audiological examination If hearing is within normal limits, primary care physician should reappraise total development and need for infant/mother stimulation program
12 to 18 months			
Vision	Amblyopia	Most parents of visually handicapped children are anxious about the child's falling and hurting him- or herself in exploration. How do you feel about this?	Corrective surgery With totally blind child, anticipatory guidance for parents regarding normal bumps and bruises as the child explores by crawling/walking Reassure parents about child's capacity to map out his/her environment
Hearing	Does not identify familiar people/objects or comprehend words Does not have comprehensible single words	Does child use words for familiar objects in the house?	Audiological examination
Communication	No single words understood by family Little comprehension of simple directions or labeled objects	Does child consistently use the same word approximation for the same object? Are new words being acquired? Does child point to familiar objects? Can he/she find familiar objects? Can he/she point to parts of the body?	

Table 6 (Cont.)

Age of Child	"Red Flags"	Questions for Parents	Interventions
18 to 36 months			
Vision, Hearing	Recheck for previous signs		
Communication	Does not show increased comprehension, acquisition of new words Does not have two-word combinations (by 30 months)		
3 to 5 years			
Vision			All children should have screening for visual acuity by primary care physician. Totally blind as well as visually impaired children should be in out-of-home settings, with sighted peers (nursery school, Head Start) to develop independence
Hearing	Any parental concerns about hearing or speech problems		All children should have competent audiometric screening (pure tone screening and impedance testing) through health department, school system, speech and hearing center NOTE: A hearing-impaired child can pass almost any gross hearing test.
Communication	Dysfluency Does not have capacity to carry on conversations or use correct pronouns and grammar of parents		Referral to speech pathologist (by 42 months)
	Hoarseness		Referral to ENT
5 to 8 years			
Vision	Behavioral problems, depression		Evaluate possible loss of vision; recheck for glaucoma, intercranial tumors, retinal deterioration Differentiation between visual acuity and visual perception
Hearing	Behavioral change		Audiometric screening as the simplest exclusionary test Annual audiometric screening for *all* children NOTE: Unilateral hearing loss is significant developmentally but usually is not picked up
Communication	Lack of consistent use of *all* speech sounds		Audiometric evaluation
	Lack of fluency in speech patterns of family		Evaluation by speech pathologist

swallowing; ability to speak; tongue movement; and some movements of the neck. These areas usually can be examined with precision, both physiologically and anatomically (see Table 6).

The next level of examination concerns motor (involuntary muscle) function. The components responsible for these functions range from high centers in the brain to the muscle itself. A disturbance at any level may cause some impairment of function. Generally, the motor system can be assessed with greater accuracy than some other parts of the nervous system. It usually can be established whether a given disturbance of motor function is due to some impairment of brain, spinal cord, peripheral nerve, or muscle. Deficits in other areas of the nervous system that participate in the control of movements (such as the basal ganglia and cerebellum of the brain) also can be identified with some accuracy.

Several reflexes are elicited during a neurologic examination. These vary from knee-jerks to pupillary reflexes of the eyes. Some reflexes, such as sucking and grasping, that are present at birth disappear with maturation.

Examination of the sensory system, difficult at any age, requires considerable cooperation on the part of the patient. It is very difficult for the yound child to cooperate sufficiently to give meaningful information, although assessment of the ability to perceive pain (pin-prick), temperature (hot-cold), light touch, position sense (direction of movement in fingers, toes, limbs), and vibration may be important in any given case. Some aspects of higher brain sensory function, such as visual, auditory, or complex exteroceptive (pain, temperature, light touch) and proprioceptive sensations (movements), are especially difficult to assess in young children. This is particularly true of those higher order sensations at that level of the brain concerned with visual and auditory perceptions, which are vital to mastery of reading and language. Many aids are available for use with these areas of function, but all such assessments require some ability of the patient to cooperate.

Other neurologic aspects. The ability of the child to read, copy geometric designs, draw figures, calculate, and perform other age-appropriate tasks must be carefully assessed. Although the physician alone can screen these functions, accurate assessment may require consultation with a qualified psychological examiner.

Other aspects of the neurologic examination should cover directionality (the ability to differentiate right from left), gait, coordination, and language and communication skills.

Laboratory Tests

When clinical observation alone is not sufficient to establish a diagnosis, laboratory tests may be a useful adjunct. To select the precise tests that are most likely to confirm a tentative diagnosis, the clinician should be familiar with certain basic "screening" instruments. For example, every child with suspected mental retardation should be tested with Phenistix for PKU; Clinitest (a reducing substance that measures galactose in galactosemia); and Labstix, which measures pH, ketones, glucose, occult blood, and protein.

Metabolic screening. If the child's history and physical examination suggest a metabolic disorder, the following compounds can be detected in blood or urine samples by simple laboratory procedures:

- Abnormal levels of amino acids can be detected by colorimetric tests, chromatography, or electrophoresis and may indicate primary amino acidurias (eg, hyperglycinuria) or secondary amino acidurias (eg, infantile cirrhosis, Lowe syndrome).

- Sugars are measured by colorimetric tests or chromatography. Abnormal levels of galactose are found in galactosemia and of pentose in pentosuria.
- Mucopolysaccharides are detected by spot tests and colorimetric tests. Increased urinary glycosaminoglycans are found in mucopolysaccharidoses (Hurler, Hunter syndromes) and related disorders (Farber disease, fucosidosis).
- Organic acids can be detected by colorimetric tests and chromatography. Abnormal levels of phenylpuruvic acid or phenyllactic acid are found in PKU, of keto acids in maple syrup urine disease, of methylmalonic acid in vitamin B dependency syndromes, of lactic acid in Leigh encephalopathy, and of uric acid in Lesch-Nyhan syndrome.

If results of any of these tests are positive, further diagnostic tests usually are required. Also, if the test results are negative but the history or physical examination suggests a specific biochemical abnormality, the physician should refer the patient for more specific enzymatic investigation.

Special Tests

The physician should complete the clinical examination, basic laboratory tests, and behavioral appraisal of the child before performing special tests or procedures to clarify the problem. Specialized studies can be valuable adjuncts in an overall clinical neurologic assessment. As with all laboratory studies, however, these tests alone generally will not resolve a given problem; they must be evaluated in terms of the overall clinical situation.

When special testing is indicated, the physician should seek out local or regional services that perform such tests and should plan to follow up on the results by bringing the parents or guardians up to date on the findings and reasons for initiating, altering, or ceasing treatments.

X-rays. Skull x-rays can be helpful in some clinical situations, particularly when possible injuries, maldevelopments of the skull, previous infections, or other factors that might contribute to calcification of brain or blood vessels or erosion of bone due to abnormal growth are involved. X-rays, however, generally are not useful in assessing disorders of learning and/or behavior.

Computer assisted tomography. A CAT scan facilitates diagnosis of hydrocephalus and other congenital anomalies and may provide accurate information regarding intracranial hemorrhage.

Ultrasonography. Ultrasonography is helpful in delineating hydrocephalus in the newborn as well as intracranial hemorrhage.

Electroencephalogram. An electroencephalogram (EEG) can be a valuable laboratory aid in assessing selected problems. Children with many clinical manifestations of nervous system diseases (eg, cerebral palsy, epilepsy, severe mental retardation) have a high incidence of EEG abnormalities; the physician must evaluate the significance of their presence or absence. The EEG does have some shortcomings when it is used to assess learning and/or behavioral difficulties.

The EEG measures only the electrical activity of the brain; it does not measure intellectual level. Additionally, the question of establishing the presence or absence of "brain damage" is often posed. Finally, abnormalities in EEG recordings mean little unless they can be related to specific clinical problems. Although many researchers have attempted to correlate EEG deviations with abnormal learning and/or behavior, each has approached the problem somewhat differently and there is little consensus.

*Assessing Diagnostic Implications and Treatability**

Phenylketonuria. One of the most common disorders, phenylketonuria (PKU), is presumed to be detected by newborn (Guthrie) blood phenylalanine tests. However, false negative reports occur and are as yet biologically unexplained. Therefore, additional laboratory confirmation of the original negative Guthrie test at the time of clinical evaluation is essential for the infant with delayed development and/or seizures of the infantile spasm type (myoclonic seizures or so-called Even a few older children with autism have been found to have PKU, unrecognized by early infant tests. Also, the child of a PKU mother untreated for high blood phenylalanine during pregnancy has more than a 95% probability of being mentally retarded (with or without PKU). A full appreciation of such second-generation problems is only now beginning to emerge.

Neurologic abnormalities. The observation of neurologic degeneration, as in an infant who is developmentally normal to six months of age and whose skills then deteriorate significantly, may suggest one of several neurodegenerative diseases characterized by a lysosomal enzyme deficiency. Tay-Sachs disease, found especially in Jewish infants, is a classic example. However, such disorders may affect any ethnic group and require at least a white blood cell lysosomal enzyme assay. Some lysosomal disorders progress so slowly over time that they give the appearance of nonprogressive (static encephalopathy) disorders. Months or years may pass before a disorder presenting with delayed development and the clinical impression of mental retardation is identified, in fact, as a progressive neurologic disorder.

---

*Prepared by Richard Allen, M.D., Professor of Pediatrics and Neurology, University of Michigan Medical School, Ann Arbor, Michigan.

Metabolic abnormalities. The association of unique clinical signs with mental retardation may provide clues to an underlying metabolic disorder. Athetoid or choreoathetoid cerebral palsy in developmentally delayed boys, accompanied by self-mutilation (such as chewing of the fingers and lips), suggests the sex-linked Lesch-Nyhan syndrome, a disorder of uric acid metabolism. Body overgrowth, especially in height, is found in homocystinuria, a disorder of methionine metabolism. Repeated bouts of ketoacidosis may be the initial clue to an underlying organic aciduria, a group of conditions that affect various levels of the metabolism of amino acids. These conditions generally require gas liquid chromatography (GLC) of biological samples to establish a diagnosis. Diseases affecting mucopolysaccharide metabolism cause a dysmorphogenesis such as that seen in Hurler syndrome.

While defects in the metabolic steps of amino acids became a model for mental retardation, presumably due to deficiencies of genetic enzymes, not all amino acidurias or amino acidemias respond to specific therapy. In some forms, amino acid abnormalities are associated with clinical symptoms but are not responsive to any presently available standard treatment. Some disorders that are associated with an increase in urine amino acids but not amino acids in blood are due to renal transport defects. Certain catastrophic metabolic disorders are associated with nonspecific biochemical (ketoacidosis) and clinical (coma) symptoms. A metabolic cause for the associated developmental delay may not be immediately apparent.

Another unusual example is a sudden cerebrovascular stroke in a child, which may suggest homocystinuria, a disorder of methionine metabolism that inexplicably results in thromboembolic occlusions. Galactosemia, a disorder of carbohydrate metabolism, also may present with severe developmental effects in the neonate along with metabolic acidosis, jaundice, and cataracts.

Table 7
Simple Urine Screening Tests

Chemical Reagents[1]	Phenylketonuria[2]	Homocystinuria	Histidinemia	Maple Syrup Urine Disease	Galactosemia
Ferric chloride[3] (also available in a commercial dip stick)	+ (dark green)	0	+	+ (black-brown)	0
2,4-dinitrophenyl-hydrazine (reacts to ketoacids)[4]	(yellow precipitate)	0	0	+	+ (related to metabolic acidosis and ketoaciduria)
Cyanide-nitroprusside (Brand Test)	0	+ (magenta)	0	0	0
Benedict's reagent for reducing substances	0	0	0	0	+ (negative glucose oxidase test)

[1]These chemical reagents are available in most routine clinical laboratories, as well as in some physicians' offices, and have been used for years for basic evaluation of a variety of urine metabolites. Such testing generally does not require special laboratory facilities.

[2]A musty odor may be recognized in the older infant or child with long-standing untreated PKU due to metabolites deriving from chronically elevated blood phenylalanine. Maple Syrup Urine Disease very early in life during acute metabolic disturbances, as well as with CNS depression, coma, and seizures, may reveal a typical maple syrup odor to random urine samples. A "sweaty feet" odor is recognized in several organic acidemias. Therefore, in addition to the odor of the urine or sweat of the patient, five simple chemical tests may help to make an initial tentative diagnosis. Plasma ammonia levels, electrolytes, quantitative amino acids in plasma and urine, and HPGLC will be required in the case of persistent clinical suspicion of an underlying metabolic disease. Some diseases, such as mucopolysaccharidosis (Hurler Disease), may be tentatively suggested by qualitative urine tests that include precipitation of random urine samples by acid albumin turbidity and also in "spot tests" that use toluidine blue or alcin blue on filter paper. However, this group of disorders is much more likely to be suspected by clinical diagnosis than by the identification in qualitative tests of urine mucopolysaccharides that are highly variable within this heterogenous group of disorders associated with mental retardation and in most dysmorphogeneses. Methylmalonic acid (MMA) also may be found in organic acidemias by qualitative urine tests.

[3]Neonatal benign tyrosinemia (often found transiently in premature infants) also will produce an evanescent green color with ferric chloride. Neonatal PKU — at least within the first few days or weeks of life — may be associated with a negative urine ferric chloride test, while the blood phenylalanine is elevated, giving a positive Guthrie test in screening programs.

[4]Organic acidurias associated with ketoacidosis in various stages may give a positive 2,4-DNPH test. However, organic acidurias characteristic of the various underlying enzyme defects generally require specialized high performance gas liquid chromatography (HPGLC).

The enormous number of retardation-related biochemical abnormalities discovered in recent years suggests that a few preliminary steps by the clinician may lead to early diagnosis before more extensive laboratory investigation is completed. The recognition of an unusual body odor, for example, or a similar odor in the urine of a mentally retarded child may be the initial step in discovering an underlying metabolic disease. Several simple tests may be performed on random urine samples that might facilitate a preliminary clinical diagnosis and initiation of treatment before the final diagnosis is made (see Table 7).

Many of these disorders respond to restriction of certain amino acids in the diet, while others are associated with acute metabolic disturbances that may require treatment. In ketoacidosis with dehydration, electrolytes and hydration are necessary, while in disorders such as maple syrup urine disease in the acute stage, peritoneal dialysis has been life-saving in some children. Other forms of metabolic disease may respond to specific cofactor supplementation. Biotin, a water-soluble vitamin, has been a valuable therapeutic intervention measure in a variety of clinical syndromes, including metabolic acidosis, neonatal seizures, and ataxia in older children. In several other vitamin responsive disorders, vitamin therapy may be useful in altering the accumulation of metabolites but may not significantly alter the clinical course of the condition (eg, homocystinuria).

The early stages of what eventually will be clinical mental retardation may present with convulsions in the infant. Symptoms may respond to therapy, such as the use of pyridoxine in the pyridoxine-dependent infant (in contrast to the pyridoxine deficiency associated with particular diets), while an underlying disturbance in amino acid metabolism requires specific loading tests, such as tryptophan in pyridoxine-dependent disorders. Standard metabolic screens in such infants would prove to be normal. In some instances, confirmation of the underlying biochemical defect may have to be delayed until after initial treatment, particularly in the catastrophically ill infant or child.

Genetic abnormalities. When a biochemical error results in failure to produce an enzyme necessary for a specific biochemical reaction, a genetic defect occurs. Not all genetic defects are inherited, but (with the exception of Down syndrome) noninherited genetic causes of mental retardation are rare.

Historically, families have been referred for genetic counseling because a family member has a definite or possible genetic condition. In such a situation, genetic counseling can help the couple assess the risk of producing a similarly affected child.

Screening for high risk. If each parent carries one normal gene and one abnormal gene (each being a heterozygote for the abnormal gene), there is a one-in-four probability that they will pass their abnormal genes to an offspring. If this occurs, the offspring will have the disease produced by the two abnormal genes.

The objective of a heterozygote screening program is to specifically and accurately identify normal individuals and couples who carry one abnormal gene so that they can obtain genetic counseling before they have children.

A good example of such a condition is Tay-Sachs disease. Approximately one in 3,600 infants among Eastern European Jewish populations is born with Tay-Sachs disease, while only one in 360,000 non-Jewish infants is affected. Approximately one in 30 healthy persons in those same Jewish populations is a heterozygote for the gene that causes Tay-Sachs disease. Thus, the frequency of the abnormal gene for Tay-Sachs disease in those populations is quite high.

Carriers of autosomal recessive genes usually are healthy and are recognized only with the delivery of a defective infant. However, recognition of the heterozygous state before conception occurs is the optimal situation.

Tay-Sachs disease, like PKU, is caused by deficiency of a certain enzyme, hexosaminidase-A, of which the blood of affected infants contains very little. Even the blood of healthy heterozygotes for the Tay-Sachs gene contains less hexosaminidase-A than that of individuals who do not carry the gene. Thus, heterozygotes for Tay-Sachs disease can be identified by a blood test. If both prospective parents are tested before they conceive and are found to be carriers of the abnormal gene, they can receive genetic counseling and consider various options concerning family planning.

Origin of abnormalities. In diagnosing an infant or young child, the physician must determine whether the condition in question is genetic or nongenetic in origin. After one affected child, the risk of recurrence is low when all of the following conditions are satisfied: (1) the family history, carefully taken, is negative; (2) both parents are free of the disorder; (3) there is no evidence of abnormal pregnancy wastage; (4) the affected child does not have any known genetically-determined condition, such as gargoylism, Tay-Sachs disease, or phenylketonuria; (5) the child and parents have no chromosomal aberrations; and (6) the mother is relatively young.

It may be extremely difficult to determine whether the cause of diagnosed mental retardation is a rare autosomal recessive disorder, an X-linked recessive disorder, or a chromosomal aberration. Therefore, certain screening tests should be used to help establish a more precise diagnosis. If family history is positive and careful investigation indicates that the disorder in the child and affected relatives is similar, the parents should be referred for genetic counseling. The physician should provide the counselor with all relevant information about family history and confirmation of the diagnosis.

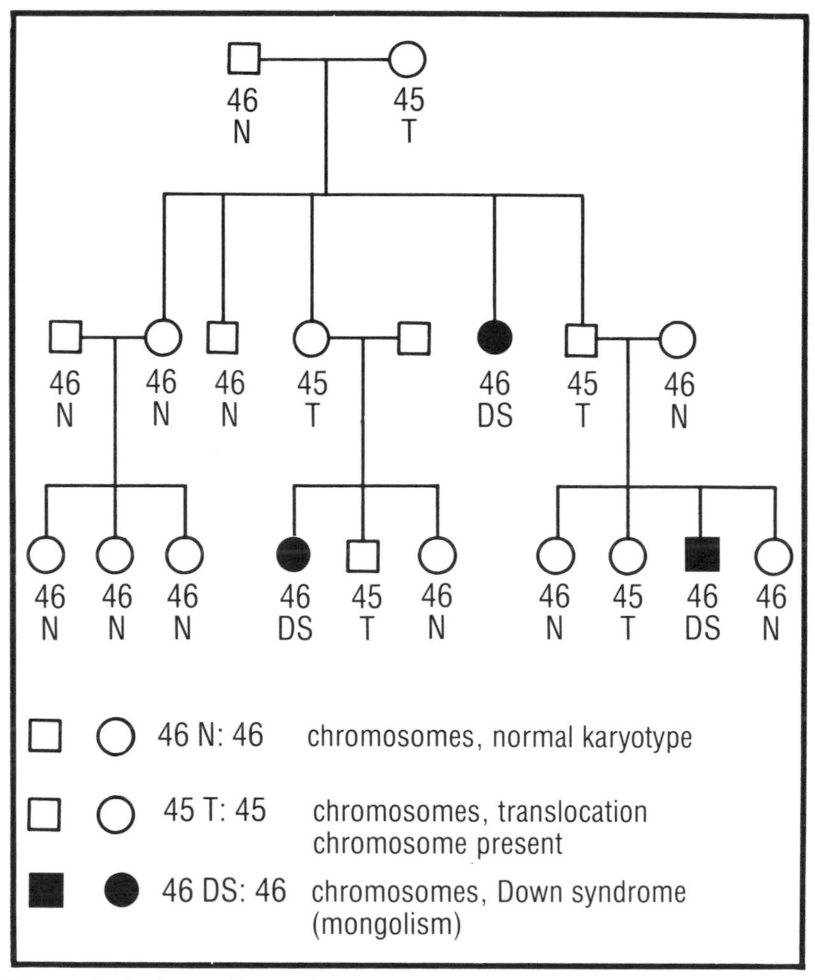

Figure A. Pedigree illustrating multiple instances of Down syndrome (mongolism) associated with translocation chromosome, eg, 14/21. Note three types of offspring from mating of normal (46 N) individual with phenotypically normal carrier parent (45 T). (Prepared by Stanley Wright, MD)

Chromosomal studies. Chromosomal studies using specialized laboratory procedures should be performed on any child with three or more congenital malformations that do not form a recognizable syndrome. Possible causes of chromosomal aberrations include genetic mutations; radiation; prenatal exposure to drugs and other chemicals;

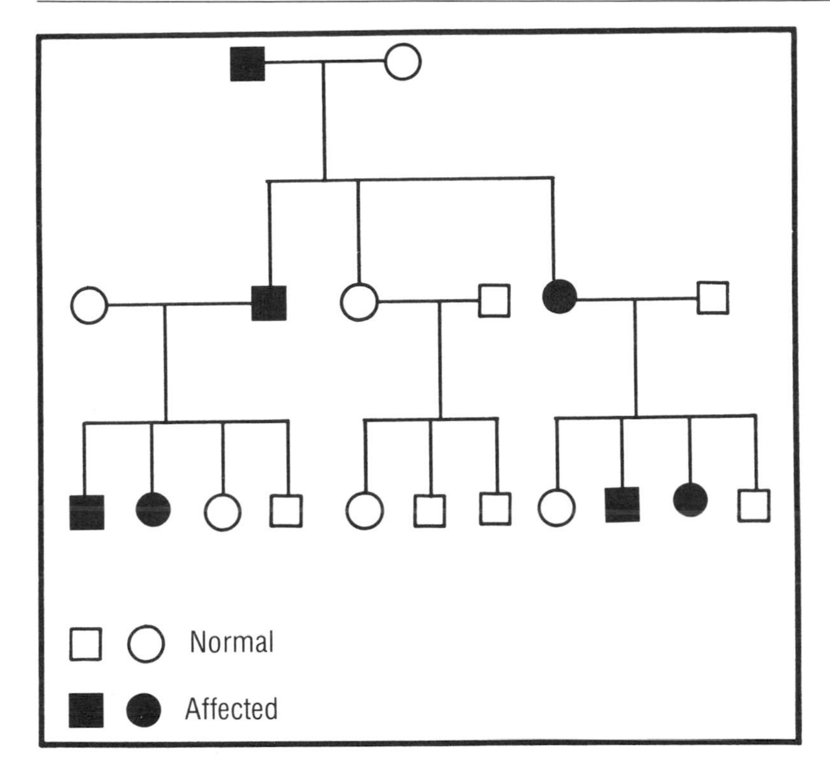

Figure B. Pedigree illustrating simple dominant inheritance, eg, Huntington chorea. Note (1) transmission of trait through affected persons; (2) both sexes equally affected; (3) appropriate ratio of 1:1 for affected to unaffected. (Prepared by Stanley Wright, MD)

viruses; autoimmune mechanisms; aged gametes (egg and sperm); and other conditions involving thermal, temporal, geographic, and (possibly) economic factors.

Down syndrome. Down syndrome is the single physical condition most often responsible for moderate and severe mental retardation. It also is the most easily recognizable syndrome. First described in 1866 by Down, this condition was often called "mongolism" because affected individuals had slanted eyes and short stature. In 1959, a third chromosome matching one of the 23 pairs was discovered in persons

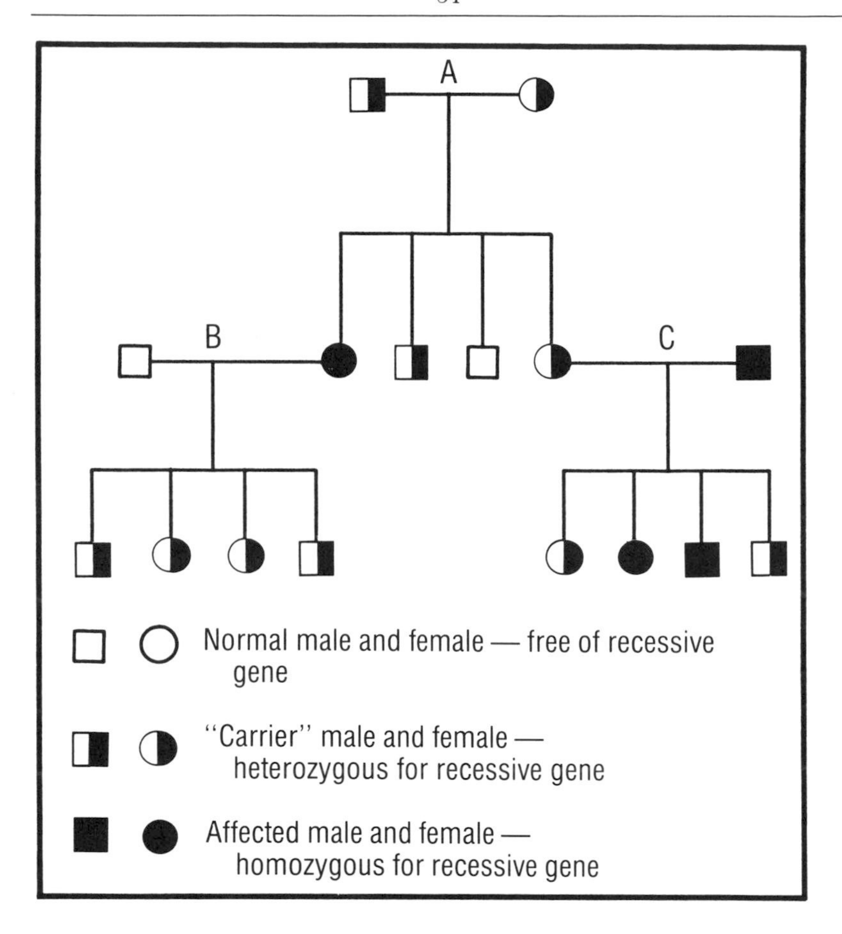

Figure C. Pedigree illustrating simple recessive inheritance, eg, phenylketonuria. "Carrier" parents of affected children have no clinical evidence of disease (A), but each child has a 25% chance of being affected. When affected individual marries person free of recessive gene (B), children will be carriers and have no clinical evidence of disease. If affected individual marries carrier (C), statistically one half of offspring will show the disease and one half will be carriers of the trait. Carrier state for a recessive gene is seldom detectable. (Prepared by Stanley Wright, MD)

affected with this syndrome. The specific pair of chromosomes involved was designated as Number 21, and the resultant condition now is frequently referred to as Trisomy 21. The individual with Down syndrome has 47 rather than 46 chromosomes, with extra material on the twenty-first chromosomal pair. Overall, about one in every 660 neonates is affected; however, the incidence of this disorder increases with maternal age.

Chromosomal studies of the affected child are indicated in every case of Down syndrome. However, on rare occasions when the physician does not have access to such studies, the parent can be informed that empirically--in cases in which the family history is normal--the probability of recurrence is in the range of 1 in 50 to 1 in 100 births. In the event that the affected child has died without these studies, chromosomal studies on both parents should be performed to rule out an inherited translocation.

'Sex' chromosomal abnormalities. Mental retardation also has been caused by abnormalities in the so-called sex chromosomes. In Klinefelter syndrome, males have an extra X chromosome and are designated XXY rather than the normal XY. The extra X chromosome gives rise to certain female secondary sex characteristics, such as breast development and immature development of the male genitalia. A typical result is mild mental retardation. Turner syndrome is a sex chromosomal disorder in females marked by the absence of an X chromosome, with attendant abnormalities in secondary sex characteristics and mild mental retardation.

Fragile-X syndrome. X-linked mental retardation involves a heterogeneous group of X-linked recessive disorders controlled by one or more genes located on the X chromosome. This group of disorders occurs more commonly in males than in females. Estimates of prevalence vary; some indicate that up to 25% of the retarded male population may be affected.

Fragile X-syndrome, the suspected cause of X-linked mental retardation in up to 33% of cases by some estimates, is a recently recognized clinical entity that takes its name from a fragile site on the X chromosome of affected individuals. In addition to mental retardation, this disorder is characterized by the following phenotypical features: macro-orchidism, prominent symphysis of the jaw, large ears, and normal to large head circumference. Early diagnosis of Fragile-X syndrome and provision of genetic counseling to affected families are essential because of the seeming frequency of this disorder in the retarded male population and its inherited nature.

Dominant and recessive genes. The physician's explanation of the difference between recessive and dominant genes often is helpful to parents. Recessive genes result in a defective child only when the same recessive gene is contributed by both parents. This process is known as "pairing." PKU, which occurs in about 1 in 13,000 births, is one condition that can result. Dominant genes rarely are involved in mental retardation. An exception is Huntington chorea, which usually is expressed in young adults and middle-aged persons. Many conditions caused by dominant genes can kill the fetus in utero or so impair the individual that he or she later cannot procreate. Another dominant gene condition, tuberous sclerosis, can have minimal effects on one generation and severe effects on the next.

For recessive disorders, there is a 25% chance of recurrence with each succeeding pregnancy. Dominant disorders generally can be recognized by transmission of the disorder through several generations, by the fact that both sexes may be affected, and by the probability that the affected child has an affected parent.

In some dominant disorders, such as tuberous sclerosis and neurofibromatosis, the parental and antecedent family history often is genetically normal. Because the disorder in these cases may be caused by a new mutation, the risk of recurrence is less than 10%. New mutations, however, should be considered only after the physician has carefully examined both parents and found no prior evidence of the disease. Even then, a situation can occur in which a parent presents no manifestations of the disease but may transmit it to half of his or her children. A sex-linked recessive trait generally can be recognized by the typical pattern of transmission, with normal females and affected males. For some autosomal recessive conditions, methods have been developed to detect carriers; Tay-Sachs disease and galactosemia are two examples.

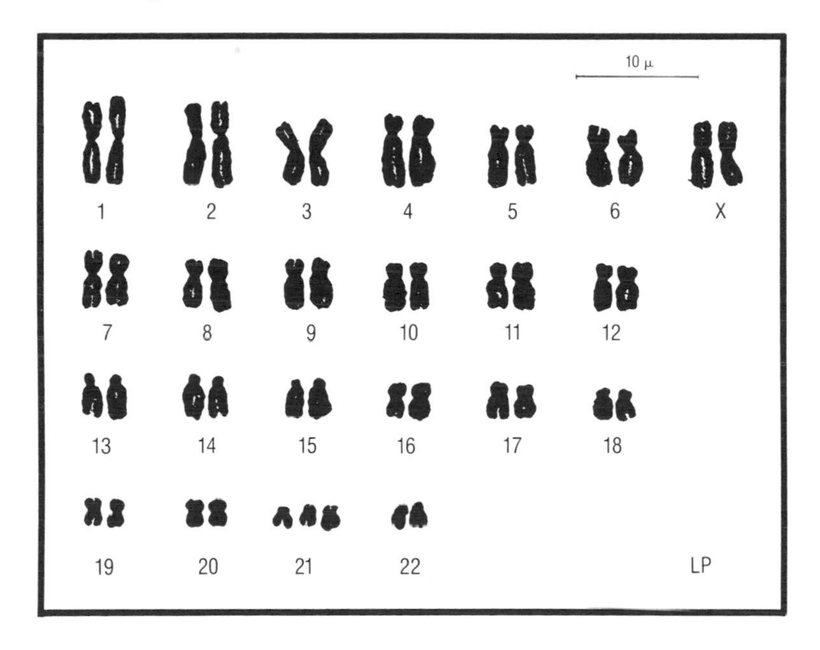

Figure D. Typical karyotype of female patient with Down syndrome, chromosome No. 47. Note trisomy 21. (Prepared by Lytt I. Gardner, MD)

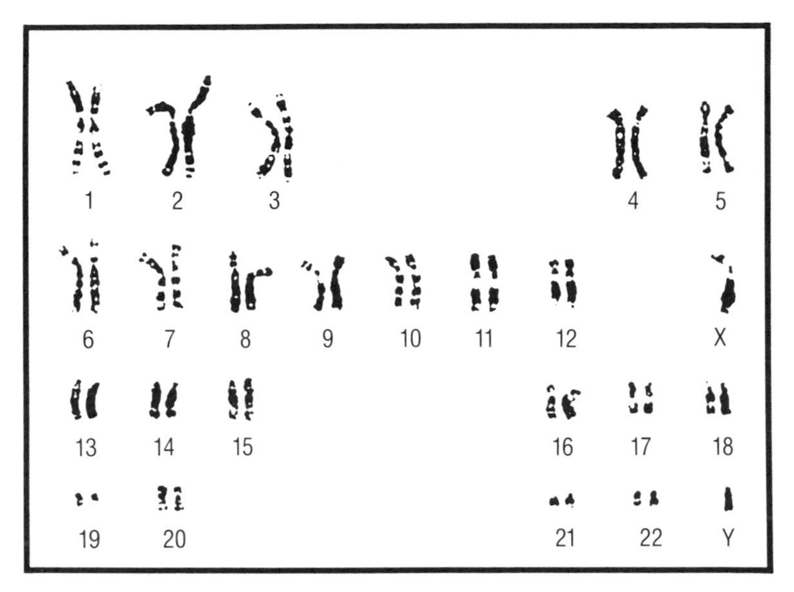

Figure E. Normal male karyotype to show Tryspin-Giemsa banding. (Figs. E and F prepared by Barbara F. Crandall, MD)

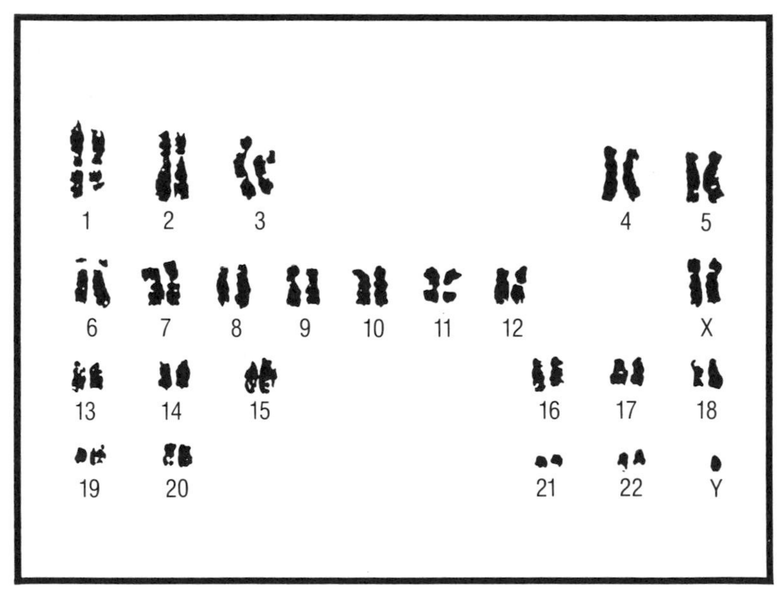

Figure F. Trypsin-Giemsa banded karyotype of patient with Klinefelter syndrome. Note XXY chromosome.

Occasionally, chromosomal studies are useful adjuncts in establishing a diagnosis of mental retardation, even though they generally are more helpful in the prevention of birth defects.

While mental retardation has associated social, economic, and political implications, the physician is a central figure in the initial diagnosis. Diagnosis not only is important in the medical management and other services provided to the mentally retarded child and his or her family; it plays a role in prevention as well. These interrelationships and the physician's position as facilitator of medical and other services will be discussed in subsequent chapters.

CHAPTER FOUR

Psychological Assessment

Psychological assessment is a complex process that must be adapted to the needs of each patient. Test scores are only one of many measures; in recent years, more importance has been assigned to factors such as social competence, motivation, and learning potential. Even so, carefully performed psychological tests can be helpful in assessing intellectual and developmental levels, and information derived from intelligence and adaptive behavior tests may be useful in establishing a diagnosis, planning treatment, and counseling both patient and family. Certainly, low intelligence scores remain an essential component of a diagnosis of mental retardation.

Intelligence and Adaptive Behavior

Intelligence is defined as the ability to learn, to recall information and use it appropriately, to gain insights and solve problems, to acquire and use language, to exercise good judgment, to discern similarities and differences, and to think abstractly.

Adaptive behavior, as defined by the American Association on Mental Deficiency, is performance in coping with environmental demands. Intelligence is expressed through a person's adaptive behavior and can be measured by observation of that behavior.

Intelligence and physical abilities are not necessarily related. Individuals who lack coordination in movement or whose hearing or sight is impaired can be highly intelligent and exhibit appropriate adaptive behavior. In appraising the behavior of such persons as a sign of intelligence, a distinction must be made between performance limitations that result from sensory or motor impediments and those that result from impaired intelligence.

Just as individuals differ from each other in height and weight, they differ in intelligence. Physical factors, such as maternal drug use and infections or injuries incurred during the prenatal or postnatal period, may impair brain structure or function and affect the development of intelligence. Psychosocial influences, such as over- or understimulation in the home environment, also may adversely influence intelligence.

Assessment of intelligence. Individuals demonstrate intelligence through successful adaptation to academic and occupational sensorimotor skills. Daily behavior cannot be observed in a standardized way, but intelligence tests that contain standardized tasks and work samples are appropriately used to assess intelligence and adaptive behavior. When these tests are administered under carefully controlled conditions, performance may be compared with norms based on the performance of many persons to yield a meaningful score. Tests are now available to assess the intelligence and adaptive behavior of individuals from infancy to old age.

Intelligence test scores are expressed as an index--the “intelligence quotient” (IQ)--that summarizes an individual’s performance or level of general intellectual functioning on a given test. Changes in IQ can occur over time, and IQ tests have certain limitations that will be discussed later in this chapter. However, an IQ score based on the results of an individually administered test is more reliable than most other scores, and it tends to remain fairly constant for most individuals over long periods.

Assessment of adaptive behavior. Adaptive behavior can be assessed informally through direct observation or by asking teachers, parents, and other care providers to describe the extent to which a person handles self-care needs, displays social amenities, takes directions, and communicates effectively.

Standardized adaptive behavior assessment tests permit clinicians to make more objective determinations than those based on unstructured interviews or limited observation. These tests not only measure an individual's ability to accomplish specific tasks in terms of typical expectations for specific ages; they also measure the individual's sense of personal responsibility, decision-making skills, choice of behaviors, and social responsibility as expressed in levels of conformity, social adjustment, and emotional maturity.

Like tests of intelligence, tests of adaptive behavior are standardized for administrative procedure and scoring. However, the scales for assessment of adaptive behavior are not as well standardized or predictive as those for intelligence tests. Nevertheless, good tests can contribute to a valid diagnosis and treatment plan.

Certain "screening" tests for adaptive behavior are commonly used in addition to intelligence tests, including the following:

Denver Prescreening Developmental Questionnaire

The Denver PDQ is a brief, valid prescreening questionnaire used to identify children who should be more thoroughly screened with the Denver Developmental Screening Test (DDST). The PDQ consists of 97 items that span the age range from 3 months to 6 years. It is completed by the parent or by an office assistant who questions the parent for two to five minutes. The scoring method produces referrals for further and more detailed screening, for which the DDST is recommended.

Denver Developmental Screening Test

The DDST is an easily administered and interpreted compilation of major universal developmental milestones organized in four segments: gross motor, fine motor, language, and personal-social. This screening device samples observable behaviors appropriate for normally developing children from birth through 6 years. It can be administered in the physician's office in about 20 minutes by a trained office assistant.

The test is useful in helping the physician identify incipient delays in the areas of development measured by the test. Designed for use as a screening instrument, the test should be regarded not as fully diagnostic but only as a guide pointing to the need for detailed evaluation of apparent weaknesses. Reliability and validity studies are reported by Frankenburg, et al. Manuals and test forms also are available in Spanish.

Gesell Developmental Schedules

The Gesell schedules are a well established method for studying mental growth of the child through the first five years of life. The schedules produce qualitative measurements of motor development, adaptive behavior, language development, and personal-social behavior. The child's performance is expressed in developmental quotients (DQs). Administration time is approximately 60 minutes for older children and less for infants. As with most tests of infant development, test-retest reliability increases with age.

Preschool Language Scale

Developed by Zimmerman, et al, this scale uses a graduated series of tasks to screen for language comprehension and speech production of children from 18 months through 7 years of age. The tasks, categorized according to 6-month age intervals, were selected and referenced from widely accepted and used measures of intelligence, development, and achievement. The test is easily administered and scored.

Alpern-Boll Developmental Profile

The Developmental Profile is an inventory of skills designed to assess a child's development from birth to pre-adolescence. Information is obtained through a parent interview, and the interviewer (evaluator) need not be a trained developmentalist. Administration time is 20 to 30 minutes. The inventory provides a profile of the child's developmental age level for particular skills according to age norms in the following four areas: physical age, self-help age, academic age, and communication age. The style and form of the profile also yield valuable impressions of parents' conceptualizations of their children and their developmental needs.

Goodenough-Harris Drawing Test (Draw-a-Person Scale)

This test, originally published in 1926, was revised by Harris in 1963. Both forms of the scale yield quick as well as fairly valid and reliable estimates of levels of intellectual functioning. Only paper and a pencil are required to administer the test. In the Harris revision, individuals are asked to draw one human figure of each sex. Points are scored for style, motor skill, and inclusion of figure details. The points are totaled to yield mental age and standard scores. This test lends itself readily for use in the physician's office, is brief, and is easily administered and scored.

The following are commonly used intelligence tests:

Stanford-Binet Intelligence Scale, Form L-M

Form L-M, a revision of the 1937 revised Stanford-Binet individual test of intelligence, is used for persons 2 years of age through adulthood. Test items are arranged on a mental age ladder so that the individual is tested only on those items most appropriate for his or her chronologic age and functional level. Test items for young children include verbal and visual recall, naming objects and pictures, perceptual discrimination, drawing, and following verbal commands. Test items at the 7-year age level and higher are primarily verbal tasks.

Scores are expressed in terms of mental age and IQ. Administration time is 60 to 90 minutes. Good validity and reliability are reported.

Bayley Scales of Infant Development

A dependable instrument for assessing early mental and psychomotor development, the Bayley Scales are intended for use with infants and young children 2 to 30 months of age. These scales, which facilitate systematic ratings of qualitative aspects of the child's behavior, can be administered in approximately 45 minutes.

Cattell Infant Intelligence Scale

Cattell's Scale, a widely-used infant test, is a downward extension of the Stanford-Binet and is organized and administered procedurally in that form. Test-retest reliabilities are poor below 9 months but improve with advancing age. It is most useful in follow-ups in which continuity with Stanford-Binet assessments is desired.

Wechsler Intelligence Scale for Children - Revised (WISC-R)

The WISC-R, a revision of the 1949 Wechsler Intelligence Scale for Children (WISC), consists of 12 tests organized into Verbal and Performance Scales. The Verbal Scale measures understanding of verbal concepts and the child's ability to respond orally. Ability to solve problems involving object manipulation or other manual response is measured by the Performance Scale. Deviation IQs are provided for the Verbal Scale, Performance Scale, and Full Scale. The IQ obtained represents the child's comparative rank and standing above or below the average performance of children in the same age group. The test is appropriate for use with children 6 through 16 years of age. Administration time is approximately 60 minutes. Good reliability and validity are reported, and the test is used extensively in schools and clinics.

Wechsler Preschool and Primary Scale of Intelligence (WPPSI)

Developed by Wechsler as a downward extension of the WISC Scale, this test follows the form and approach used in other Wechsler scales. It is designed for use with children 4 through 6.5 years of age. Verbal, Performance, and Full scale IQs are produced, and Verbal IQs correlate highly with those of Stanford-Binet. Administration time is approximately 60 minutes.

Implications of Test Results

While there is agreement that IQ tests offer a reasonable indication of an individual's abilities, such tests have distinct limitations. For example, results may be affected by testing situations or choice of examiners. Variations attributable to differences in the standardization norms of different test instruments or to changes between editions of the same scale can lead to misinterpretation. A child's classroom behavior may not be consistent with the test results. Finally, test results are not equally applicable to all children; racial or cultural biases often are built into them.

For these reasons, the results of one IQ test do not constitute a diagnosis. Scores are merely a record of one individual's performance on a given test at a given time. There is the danger of inappropriately labeling a child on the basis of a single observation. Parents, teachers, and others may begin to treat the child as retarded, reinforce the perception of retardation, and cause the child to perform even more poorly on subsequent tests.

Nor should an IQ test be the determining factor in management, lest a child be assigned--even for a short time--to a program above or below his or her potential. In addition to obtaining an IQ score, the physician should confer with the psychologist responsible for testing to obtain a more balanced perspective on the child.

Other psychological and developmental tests have similar strengths and weaknesses. One drawback to some psychological reports is that they describe what the child cannot do rather than what he or she can do. The latter is more important, because the physician will want to plan a therapeutic approach based on the child's assets and abilities.

Because scales that measure adaptive behavior are not as well standardized as those available for intelligence, a great deal of judgment is involved in interpreting the results. However, as a measure of adaptive behavior, these tests may help delineate an individual's impairment.

Parents' reports may not be consistent with cognitive test results. Parents sometimes claim more than psychological tests reveal. In such cases, the physician must weigh all of the information, assess the child's adaptation, and make a diagnosis based on behavior as well as test scores after conferring with the psychologist and other involved professionals. When there is a discrepancy between reports of parents and those of professionals, the physician may defer judgment until he or she has a chance to observe the child for a while under treatment.

Because psychological tests have varied purposes, valid psychological assessments require the use of other measures. Primary care physicians who are concerned with child development problems should have access to testing facilities and psychologists who specialize in such tests, as well as a working knowledge of various developmental and psychological tests.

CHAPTER FIVE

Medical Management

Because it takes time to make a comprehensive diagnosis, to assess developmental progress, and to arrive at recommendations, the initial evaluation of a child in and of itself is of limited value. Continuity of care is essential. A chronic disorder requires a succession of segments of care attuned to the readiness of both child and parents. Such an approach not only fits the style of most primary care clinicians but also affords a degree of structure for parents. In addition, management of the psychological aspects of mental retardation calls for the kind of trusting relationship between patient and physician that can evolve only over time.

The physician should be accessible to both child and family in the event an urgent need arises. Return visits should be scheduled routinely, during which parents (and the child, as appropriate) have opportunities to talk with the physician about how things are going, develop a trusting relationship that permits sharing of problems and worries, ask questions about developmental progress and physical care, and help clarify the ongoing nature of the problem.

As the lead professional toward whom the retarded child and his or her parents often turn, the physician will want to confer with family members, teachers, psychologists, social workers, and others. If the patient is an adult, the physician should be aware of his or her living arrangements and educational progress or employment activities. In some cases, the physician may function in a more limited role. After a plan of management has been outlined, appropriate medical services may be provided by the physician, while other professionals (eg, teachers, psychologists, social workers) may be asked to assume primary responsibility for the patient.

Focus on Families

When preparing to tell a couple that their child is mentally retarded, the physician faces a dilemma regarding how much he or she should say, when it should be said, and in what manner.

One factor is the degree of certainty of the diagnosis. After the birth of a child with Down syndrome, for example, the physician should act promptly to inform the parents. With an infant whose development may be marginally slow, on the other hand, developmental progress can be discussed with the family over time in appropriate sequence.

Another significant factor is the parents' level of emotional maturity. Their ability to accept the diagnosis and adjust to the problem can be assessed from the realism of their perceptions, the appropriateness of their expectations, their concern with current rather than distant problems, how preoccupied they are with what might have been, the pertinence of their questions, how they utilize advice, the quality of their relationship with the child and one another, and the degree of denial they exhibit.

Regardless of the parents' emotional maturity, a diagnosis of mental retardation will be followed by mourning the "loss" of an anticipated "perfect" child. These parents have a predictable sequence of psychological reactions, including shock, denial, anger, and guilt. One of the physician's most difficult tasks is dealing with parents who seem unaware of or deny their child's condition or who react with fear and hostility to any attempt to help them face reality. The physician's sensitivity, subtlety, and skill can help parents bear the shattering impact of the diagnosis and contribute to their realistic adaptation during the long period of adjustment that must follow.

The physician should be prepared for secondary problems that sometimes accompany mental retardation. For example, otherwise resourceful mothers and fathers may surprisingly seem uncertain about what to do or may focus on relatively inconsequential matters. In other cases, their child rearing practices may become distorted because of depression, anxiety, ambivalence, inability to cope, and an undue focus on the child's condition without regard for the child as a person. There may be lack of communication between the parents, and the family may find itself socially isolated.

Visits during which parents have a chance to express their anxieties to a physician who listens, understands, and has the ability to inspire confidence are of great therapeutic value, as is the physician's assurance that what the parents did or failed to do had no bearing on the child's mental retardation. While they may express disappointment that there is no cure, most parents will feel confident in the physician's care and appreciate the help and support he or she offers.

Although some families can be strengthened, others become severely strained by the process of diagnosis and treatment planning. The seemingly unending demands of frequent visits to the physician and consultants, of costly laboratory tests and related expenses, may bring on physical and psychological fatigue and economic hardship. Resentment and fear, or simply lack of information, can lead to worrisome, demanding, and querulous behavior in which blame is projected on the child, the spouse, or the physician.

Even the most mature and well integrated parents find it difficult to cope with both their own feelings and the needs of their child. The new problem almost always alters their lives in some ways; the changes depend in large part on what has gone before. Some parents abandon all discipline and become overprotective and overindulgent; others redouble control or become punitive and rejecting. While siblings may resent the mentally retarded child's special attention and privileges, they also may be disturbed about his or her "special condition" and feel guilty that they may have somehow wished or caused the problem to occur.

Initial goals with parents. Management of mental retardation is complex and requires an awareness of the various services that the mentally retarded person will need throughout life. These pertain--but are not limited--to health, education, vocation, and living arrangements. There is no single source of guidance for all of these needs. Insofar as possible, a major goal for the physician is to help parents develop their capabilities and assume responsibility for effective case management. If parents are to cope, they must increasingly take on this role.

Early steps in management are to interpret to parents the results of diagnostic studies, begin parent education, and work with the family to develop a regimen consistent with the child's needs and the availability of services. Educating parents about the child's condition should be the physician's primary concern at this time; the greatest source of emotional disturbance in parents is uncertainty--not knowing what has happened and wondering what can be done.

Parents' acceptance of their child's mental retardation is a slow and emotionally painful process. Long after the initial diagnosis, they may continue to feel guilt, shame, and sorrow as they wonder why they have a retarded child. The physician must attempt to answer their often unspoken questions, such as: What is mental retardation? What are its implications for my child? What special needs will he or she have? In what ways is my child like and different from other children?

The physician's attitude during the initial management period is critical and may determine his or her future role in the child's treatment as well as influence the parents' attitude. Parental dissatisfaction at this point sometimes results in "shopping around" for physicians. Yet, the parent who "pesters" the physician most after the initial shock may be the one who makes a satisfactory long-term adjustment.

It is desirable for both parents to be present during the initial interpretation session. This not only reduces the chances of misunderstanding but also provides clues to the parental relationship that will be valuable in future management. Sometimes this approach also helps unite the parents to meet the continuing stress of coping with a mentally retarded child. The child's development may suffer if the parents' emotional attitudes or family interactions are distorted. While their child's needs for love and acceptance are the same as those of a nonretarded child, parents must be made aware of differences in emotional, intellectual, and social development.

The physician should present factual information, emphasizing the child's strengths and potentials along with handicaps and vulnerabilities. In a sympathetic manner, he or she must try to give honest, understandable information about the diagnosis and prognosis. To the parents of the patient, opinions of the primary care physician may seem to differ from those of other health professionals, friends, and relatives. In such instances, the physician should discuss differences of opinion and take the time to weigh all factors.

Ongoing appraisals for parents. During a continuing relationship that is focused on care and management, parents should be given an appraisal of their child's probable rate of development. This will help them to adjust their concept of developmental milestones (eg, sitting, walking, talking) and to begin to teach the child self-care skills, such as feeding and toilet training, at appropriate times. Advice from specific therapists may assist parents in approaching such aspects of daily care. Relatively simple suggestions about everyday care may make the difference between the ability of parents to manage a retarded child and their complete frustration.

Long-term counseling. Long-range planning becomes possible when physician and parents have come to terms with their own feelings.

In planning, the physician will want to take into consideration the disruptive effect of mental retardation on family life. Retardation also may bring with it heavy financial expenses and pose difficult problems in planning for future pregnancies. The family may feel stigmatized and isolated from the community. A family with high intellectual aspirations may find it difficult to accept a child with impaired intelligence.

The physician continues to play an active role in recommending general problem-solving techniques. Because of a close relationship with the family, the physician often can point out to parents the strengths they are displaying in coping with their problem. Such approval encourages additional effort. During the mentally retarded individual's lifetime, the physician may continue to provide important opportunities for parents to discuss their feelings as crises arise. Parents often can reduce the intensity of their anxiety by sharing it with the physician. Additionally, if the physician has trained the parents to be effective case managers for their child's condition, they will be able to deal with most nonmedical situations without much direct help from the physician. They will be acquainted with various school and social services and will know the channels through which their child's needs can be fulfilled.

The physician's ultimate goals in parent counseling are to help parents accept the child and his or her disorder as a nonstressful part of the family's life, enable the family to plan objectively without undue emotional strain, and help them feel satisfied in the knowledge that they have contributed in every way possible to developing the potential of their child.

The physician should encourage parents to seek additional sources of help for themselves in the community, such as local parent support groups. By talking with other parents, families find that their problems are not unique. (More on resources for parents is included in Appendix C.)

Additionally, the physician may occasionally give practical, specific suggestions to parents at specific developmental stages. For example, the mother may be helped to understand that her own anxieties and tensions might be contributing to the child's disruptive behavior, and that she can interrupt the cycle of such behavior by enforcing firm limits and remaining calm and consistent in discipline.

Emotional Reactions of Physicians

Physicians also react emotionally to the problems of mental retardation. Recognizing this fact, they should be aware that their personal outlook can affect the content and manner of their counseling. For example, the physician who identifies too closely with parents and feels that they indeed have an intolerable burden may fail to deal realistically with the problems of long-term management. Or, sensing the parents' denial and hostility, the physician may react with denial and hostility. Also, faced with the parents' need for immediate answers or insistence that something be done at once, the physician may be provoked into acting in a blunt or seemingly uninterested way.

General Aspects of Medical Management

Infancy and childhood. Parents may have to modify usual child-care practices for their mentally retarded child. Systematic habit training has much to offer the handicapped child, but each step will be slow and repetition is important. Breaking a complex task into small steps, providing a setting in which the child can successfully perform the act, and immediately rewarding a correct response increase learning. The child learns by mimicry as well as practice to perform daily activities such as dressing, eating, and brushing teeth. Walkers, bars, and other supportive devices may be used to teach walking. Toilet training is best accomplished by taking the child to the toilet at specific intervals, as is recommended for nonretarded children.

Most communities have special services for preschool retarded children in accordance with Public Law 94-142, the Education for All Handicapped Children Act, and the physician should make appropriate referrals (see Chapter VI, Other Service Needs). Socialization of the child may improve in programs that emphasize small group activities and concentrate on self-help and personal skills. Gross motor development may be enhanced by physical therapy in combination with training or socialization programs. School readiness and perceptual motor skills can be sharpened in special preschool programs that emphasize space and time orientation, reading readiness, and the language and social skills required for primary special education programs.

Elementary schools offer various programs for different degrees of impairment, including those for the severely handicapped. The physician should be prepared to inform parents about these resources. Once a diagnosis has been made, a broad range of services mandated by P.L.94-142 may be accessed through the local public school system (see Chapter VI, Other Service Needs).

Psychosocial support for families may be available through community mental health centers, public welfare agencies, and the community-based Association for Retarded Citizens (ARC). Parents and siblings of mentally retarded children may need regular respites from the intense demands involved in their care.

Adolescence. As at other ages, problems in adolescence vary with the severity of the young person's intellectual deficit. Thus, mildly retarded individuals face problems similar to those of the average adolescent, although many such problems occur at a later chronologic age.

These years are crucial, as the young person attempts to adjust to society and becomes increasingly aware of his or her disability. Problems in relating to the family may intensify because of parental concern over the child's social life, which often becomes more difficult at the junior high level. While family members may not always be able to verbalize these concerns, the physician should be alert to them.

In adolescence, behavior problems are common. These may stem from a striving for identity or may represent an expression of hostility and frustration toward a society that taxes the young person's abilities with increasing demands. Academic, social, and athletic failures are common. Delinquent behavior may occur. Because of the diversity of the social, educational, and adjustment problems in this age group, the physician will find it helpful to work with other professional disciplines and with social service agencies.

As the adolescent matures, planning for prevocational and vocational training as well as for independent living become necessary. Programs and management depend on the degree of retardation and social adaptation as well as on the extent and quality of resources in the community.

In the severely and profoundly retarded patient, sex drive may be quite limited. Mildly retarded individuals usually have normal sex drives but lack judgment, which might lead to difficulties. Learning about sex is part of developing appropriate social competence and behavior. Education of mentally retarded adolescents in these matters should be handled in much the same way it is with other young persons. Teaching about sex and preparation for family life is a developmental phenomenon, and information should be given by parents and physician within the capacity of the adolescent to understand at the time he or she raises questions. More consideration should be given to mental age and ability to comprehend than to chronologic age.

Adulthood. Twenty years ago, most mentally retarded persons who lived beyond childhood spent the remainder of their lives in institutions.

Today, many retarded children are surviving into adulthood and living in community settings. These individuals present a formidable challenge to primary care physicians, whose education and training may not have prepared them to deal with retarded adults.

This emerging class of patients may present with a variety of special problems. Approximately 15% of individuals with Down syndrome between ages 30 and 50 exhibit hypothyroidism. Prompt diagnosis and appropriate hormone replacement therapy can successfully combat the lethargy characteristic of these patients.

Persons with Down syndrome also are susceptible to degenerative arthritis of the cervical spine and intervertebral discs. In the patient who suddenly develops gait disturbances, pain while walking, or localized neck pain or torticollis, vertebral slippage should be suspected.

Perhaps the most publicized late complication of Down syndrome is the occurrence of pathologic changes associated with Alzheimer disease. Almost all Down patients over age 35 display some symptoms, and those between ages 40 and 60 show a measurable loss of memory and intellectual function.

Mentally retarded adult women often have undetected gynecologic problems. For example, secondary amenorrhea may be associated with serious disorders such as uncorrected congenital heart defects, adult cyanotic heart disease, or chronic pulmonary disease. In women with Down syndrome, heavy menstrual flow may be linked to undetected thyroid dysfunction.

In addition to these problems, mentally retarded women may not know how to protect themselves from unwanted pregnancy or sexual abuse. The physician should be prepared to answer questions and offer advice concerning contraception and genetic counseling, or make appropriate referrals.

Other problems common to mentally retarded adults include seizures as a result of brain damage, compromised pulmonary function resulting from restriction of physical activity, a higher risk of infection from diseases against which these individuals were not immunized as children, and higher than normal incidences of periodontal disease and obesity.

The acceptance or rejection a mentally retarded individual experiences from childhood on, as well as the degree of independence he or she is encouraged to assume, influences personality, skill in interpersonal relations, and potential for emotional and social adaptation and good work habits. Physicians who counsel patients effectively in these matters can enhance their prospects for rehabilitation, independent living, and employment. When a retarded adult becomes employed, the encouragement and support of the physician who has known the individual for a long time may impart additional confidence to help him or her keep the job.

Aging. Mildly retarded older adults share the problems of much of the aging population. Many continue to live in the community, some with their families and some independently. Those who are more substantially impaired may live in sheltered environments. Overall health, memory, vision, and motor capacities diminish to varying degrees. Problems of nutrition and hygiene may increase with advancing age. In addition to the shared problems of all older adults, mentally retarded seniors have their own ongoing special needs and require the assistance of family or community members for a varying number of personal tasks.

Aging mentally retarded individuals need continuing medical care coordinated with community services. Their particular needs may warrant placement in a nursing home or other special care facility.

As with medical management of other mentally retarded patients, the physician will want to be familiar with facilities in the community that can provide sheltered care for the aging retarded individual if needed.

Selected Aspects of Medical Care

Mentally retarded persons, especially the more severely impaired, may require more general health care and supervision than nonretarded individuals. Immunizations for prevention of infectious diseases should be given routinely, as they are to all children. Frequent visits should be scheduled for well-child care. During these visits, the bond between physician and patient/family can be strengthened.

Diet. Attention to diet is important. Prevention of obesity in retarded children often is overlooked. Obesity can result from lack of physical activity, improper diet, or both. Some parents become overindulgent with retarded children and may disregard the need for good nutrition. Many parents of obese retarded teenagers find it difficult to place them on reducing diets. Counseling parents of retarded infants or toddlers about proper nutrition and emphasizing the importance of physical activity may help prevent obesity later in life.

Infections. Irritability in mentally retarded children may be caused by hidden infections. Poor dietary and hygienic habits heighten chances for nutritional anemia or intestinal parasitic diseases. These factors (as well as a possible immunologic deficit, as seen in Down syndrome) may lower the individual's resistance to disease and lead to frequent, repeated infections.

Physical fitness. The physician should encourage physical activity and fitness as beneficial to general health and as aids to socialization. This is especially important for retarded children who have associated physical handicaps.

Dental care. Dental care and hygiene often are neglected in the general health care of retarded persons, particularly those with Down syndrome. Lack of dental care in mentally retarded children leads to poor oral hygiene, excessive dental decay, and gingivitis. Except in Down syndrome, the incidence of caries is about the same as that in nonretarded children. However, once initiated, the decay tends to progress more rapidly and destructively. This may be related to a diet poor in protein and high in carbohydrates, as well as to the tendency of parents and other relatives to allow these children to overindulge in sweets.

Physicians may notice the build-up of thick, tenacious microbial colonies and carbohydrate-containing debris on the teeth of such children, as well as halitosis. Microbial masses are inhabited by cariogenic microorganisms (usually streptococci), resulting in severe and deep carious lesions, and also by toxin-producing microorganisms that cause severe and progressive gingivitis leading to periodontal diseases--especially in children with Down syndrome.

The physician who notes such conditions during a physical examination should refer the patient for appropriate dental care. Dentistry for patients with almost all forms of mental retardation is possible, regardless of the severity of the individual's condition. If the patient cannot be treated normally in the dentist's office, all dental procedures can be accomplished under light general anesthesia. Preventive and corrective dental care should be initiated as early as possible.

Treatment of seizures. Many severely and profoundly retarded persons have epilepsy, and their resulting problems--often severe and complex--reflect considerable disturbance of brain function. Management of these seizures often is more difficult than that of typical seizures in nonretarded persons. Close neurologic monitoring and medical follow-up are essential.

Physical and occupational therapy. Physical and occupational therapy may be helpful for some individuals. Early application of neurodevelopmental techniques, especially in very young infants, may prevent some abnormal muscle tone and incoordination. Parents should be taught to manipulate the limbs of infants to stimulate movement. As young people mature, occupational therapy may provide them with some skills that can be applied to vocational training.

Hearing and speech problems. Hearing and speech deficiencies are common in mentally retarded persons. Recently developed techniques, including the use of brainstem auditory evoked responses (BAERS), can detect auditory impairment in early infancy. Mentally retarded children can benefit from the use of properly fitted hearing aids. During preschool and early school years, evaluation and guidance regarding the need for speech and language therapy should be obtained from specialists. Retarded children often have articulatory defects as well as other speech impairments.

Motor skills. Some more severely retarded individuals need special motor skills training. Unlike deficient language, motor disabilities are not necessarily concomitant with retardation. Many of the same kinds of treatment and training that apply to the nonretarded are needed by retarded persons to develop gross and fine motor skills. The degree of mental retardation will govern approaches to the use and complexity of instructions; verbal instructions suitable for nonretarded individuals may have to be modified or supplemented by demonstration.

Social skill development. Although educational and physical education programs have included some recreational activities and social skills training, focus on this area by specially trained staff is important. Most programs feature recreation specialists, adaptive physical educators, and trainers in interpersonal skills and group social activities. Instruction in social and leisure skills takes place within groups.

Programs are designed to help mentally retarded persons live as independently as possible and develop and maintain social skills they can use in a variety of social settings.

Behavioral Difficulties and Use of Psychotropic Drugs

Retarded individuals are at high risk for developing psychiatric and behavioral disorders of all types. Psychoactive drugs can ameliorate the undesirable symptoms of associated behavioral and psychiatric disorders and enhance the efficacy of efforts in education, behavior modification, and physical and vocational rehabilitation. For example, educational and vocational activities are difficult to implement with retarded persons who are grossly hyperactive, distractible, and inattentive. Certain psychoactive agents may alleviate some of these symptoms so that primary treatment modalities are more effective. However, these substances should be used with caution in the mentally retarded patient because of their potential for harmful side effects and for abuse.

Mentally retarded patients with psychiatric illnesses respond to psychopharmacotherapy as do nonretarded patients who exhibit similar disorders. For example, manic episodes may be moderated dramatically by lithium and depressive episodes by tricyclic antidepressants. Schizophrenia can be treated with the phenothiazines and other antipsychotic drugs.

Rational drug therapy. A complete diagnostic evaluation as outlined in Chapter III should precede initiation of any pharmacologic therapy. In the course of the physical examination, particular emphasis should be placed on the central nervous system. A baseline assessment should be made of all target functions that are likely to be affected by the use of psychoactive drugs. This is important, because certain medications that may help control behavior also may produce unwanted results, such as adversely affected school performance

In selecting a psychopharmacologic agent, the physician should consider first and foremost its safety and efficacy for the symptomatology to be treated. A traditional and well accepted drug is recommended as a first choice rather than a new drug of the same pharmacologic class. In most cases, the initial dose of a medication should be as small as possible. Generally, the medication will have to be carefully titrated until clinical improvement is noted or until side effects occur that necessitate decreasing the dosage or discontinuing use of the agent. The physician's clinical judgment and information from other individuals who observe the patient must be carefully balanced in titrating the medication. Ratings of behavior, such as attention span and perceptual speeds, that were taken at baseline should be made at regular intervals along with measurements of learning, height, weight, and psychologic and neurologic functioning.

In determining the optimal dosage of a given drug, the physician must treat each case individually, since comparable doses of the same drug in persons of the same body weight and age may differ significantly in blood concentration. Usually, mentally retarded individuals on long-term psychoactive drug therapy should be given a drug-free trial for a specified period during the course of treatment. No psychoactive medication should be used longer than necessary to control the clinical symptoms. Even when a psychoactive agent has been shown to be effective in ameliorating such symptoms, the physician should continue efforts to confirm the diagnosis, seek possible causes of the emotional or behavioral disorder that is being treated, and use all nonpharmacologic means to minimize it.

Other effects of psychotropic agents. In addition to improving the outcome of certain diseases and disorders, pharmacologic agents usually have important effects on physiologic systems of the body, activity level, cognitive functioning and performance, academic achievement, behavior, personality, and mood. These parameters can be measured by a variety of methods (ie, physical examination, observation, different types of electrical and mechanical instruments).

Classification of Psychotropic Drugs

The psychotropic drugs can be grouped according to their effects on the central nervous system (see Table 8 for generic and trade names of the major drugs in each class).

Antipsychotics. Antipsychotics are a very useful adjunct in the treatment of "thought disorders" in nonretarded individuals. Those most commonly used in mentally retarded persons are the phenothiazines and the butyrophenone, haloperidol. The "psychoses" most commonly associated with mental retardation are infantile autism and childhood onset pervasive developmental disorder; these do not necessarily respond to antipsychotic drugs as well as do similar psychoses in nonretarded persons. The more potent (and usually less sedating) antipsychotics (eg, fluphenazine, haloperidol) are more effective than the less potent and generally more sedating antipsychotics. Mentally retarded individuals appear to have a propensity toward atropine psychosis as well, another reason to preferentially use one of the more potent antipsychotics in these patients.

Antidepressants and antimanic agents. The established clinical indications for use of antidepressants in nonretarded persons include the affective disorders. These agents also can be of significant benefit in phobic disorders, chronic anxiety states, and substance abuse disorders as well as in bulimia and anorexia nervosa. Little evidence exists that behavioral and cognitive improvement occurs in mentally retarded patients receiving these drugs unless a diagnosis of, for example, recurrent major depression has been made.

Lithium is used in nonretarded persons in the treatment of bipolar disorder. Again, in the absence of a diagnosis such as bipolar disorder,

Table 8
Classification of Representative Psychotropic Drugs

Therapeutic Classification	Generic Name	Trade Name(s)
Antipsychotics	*Phenothiazines*	
	chlorpromazine	Thorazine
	thioridazine	Mellaril
	fluphenazine	Prolixin, Stelazine
	Butyrophenone	
	haloperidol	Haldol
	Thioxanthene	
	thiothixene	Navane
	Dibenzoxazepine	
	loxapine	Loxitane
	Dihydroindolone	
	Molindone	Moban
Antidepressants	*Heterocyclics*	
	imipramine	Tofranil
	desipramine	Norpramin, Pertofrane
	amitriptyline	Elavil, Endep
	nortriptyline	Aventyl, Pamelor
	doxepin	Adapin, Sinequan
	trimipramine	Surmontil
	protriptyline	Vivactil
	maprotiline	Ludiomil
	trazodone	Desyrel
	Monoamine Oxidase Inhibitors	
	tranylcypromine	Parnate
	phenelzine	Nardil
	isocarboxazid	Marplan
Antimanic Agents	lithium	Cibalith-S, Eskalith, Lithane, Lithonate
	Anticonvulsants	
	phenytoin	Dilantin
	carbamazepine	Tegretol
	clonazepam	Klonopin
CNS Stimulants	dextroamphetamine	Dexedrine
	methamphetamine	Desoxyn
	methylphenidate	Ritalin
	pemoline	Cylert

the effects of lithium on the apparent depressive symptomatology and aggressive behavior of mentally retarded persons are not established.

Anticonvulsants. Anticonvulsants often are used to treat mentally retarded individuals who have seizure disorders. Some anticonvulsants, especially phenytoin, carbamazepine, and clonazepam, recently have been used for their antimanic action and in the treatment of lithium-resistant bipolar disorder as well as in atypical bipolar disorder. These drugs might be considered for use in a mentally retarded person who has lithium-resistant bipolar disorder.

CNS Stimulants. CNS Stimulants are used as adjuncts to other remedial measures in nonretarded children with attention-deficit disorder and conduct disorders. However, they have not been used widely in mentally retarded persons except for the treatment of attention deficit disorder with hyperactivity. Even in these individuals, some researchers have found that stimulants decrease the rate of learning. A limited field of attention (overfocusing) may be narrowed even further by the action of these agents.

Antianxiety agents and hypnotics. These agents are effective for anxiety disorders in nonretarded adults and have some usefulness in treating insomnia and other sleep disorders. However, some studies suggest that they may actually increase undesirable behavior in mentally retarded individuals by provoking paradoxical reactions, such as aggressive behavior. Because of the complexity of these clinical manifestations, practitioners should be cautious in their use of antianxiety agents and hypnotics pending the results of further research.

Controversial Therapies*

Chronic problems, such as learning disabilities, often instigate novel therapies that become controversial by their broad claims of efficacy

*Adapted from Golden GS: Controversial therapies. *Pediatr Clin North Am* 31:459-469, 1984.

and, despite the highly variable nature of the problems, by being presented as global remedies. It is only fair to state that such therapies are neither right nor wrong simply because they are controversial.

Controversial therapies can be defined operationally by certain shared characteristics: (1) The theory on which the therapy is based is novel and not completely consistent with modern scientific knowledge; (2) the new treatment is presented as effective for a broad range of problems that often are not rigorously defined; (3) because the treatment usually relies on the use of "natural" substances (eg, vitamins) or is based on dietary therapy, exercises, or simple manipulations of the body, it is claimed that there is no possibility of adverse effects; (4) the initial presentation is often, but not always, presented in a publication other than a peer-reviewed scientific journal; (5) controlled studies that do not support the new treatment are discounted as having been improperly performed or biased, because the "medical establishment" is unwilling to accept novel ideas; and (6) lay organizations develop and support use of the treatment, proselytize new members, and become socially active in attempting to develop special interest legislation and regulations.

Diet and hyperactivity. The hypothesis developed by Feingold states that certain food additives and colorings produce a syndrome of learning disability and hyperactivity in a group of susceptible children. This reaction is purportedly a nonimmunologic sensitivity in patients who are genetically different from the general population. It was Feingold's opinion that up to half of affected children show dramatic improvement in their learning and behavior if these substances are removed from their diet and that dietary infractions lead to a rapid return of symptoms.

Data yielded by clinical and experimental studies suggest that a small subset of hyperactive children may respond adversely to one or more artificial dietary additives. However, they indicate that this effect involves only a limited number of children, is inconsistent and difficult to reproduce, and usually is of small magnitude. There is no physical danger inherent in an additive-free diet, so long as attention is paid to basic nutritional principles. But introduction of dietary therapy is not without costs, both monetary and in terms of time commitment, and potential stresses on the child and family must be weighed. Other aspects of medical care may become an issue. For example, the family may refuse to give the child needed medications because of attempts to avoid additives and all "unnatural" substances.

A National Institutes of Health Consensus Development Conference on Defined Diets and Hyperactivity was cautious in its conclusions on this subject. While the conference suggested that "initiation of a trial of dietary treatment or continuation of a diet in patients whose families and physicians perceive benefits may be warranted," it did not discuss the ethical and scientific aspects of what essentially are empirical clinical trials of unproven methods.

Megavitamin therapy. The concept of genetotrophic disease, introduced by Williams and co-workers in 1950, postulates that certain individuals have specific genetic abnormalities that produce increased requirements for highly specific nutrients. Failure to obtain adequate amounts of the required substance produces a disease state. The vitamin-responsive aminoacidurias are examples of such conditions.

This general concept was applied to a theory of the biochemical basis of schizophrenia by Hoffer and Osmond, and a treatment protocol using niacin, pyridoxine, and vitamin C was developed. Major studies sponsored by the American Psychiatric Association and the Canadian Psychiatric Association were unable to find evidence supporting the hypothesis.

The term "orthomolecular psychiatry" was introduced by Pauling in 1968 to describe this type of therapy. The paper was speculative and was not based on any studies in the area of behavioral abnormalities carried out by the author.

The use of orthomolecular or megavitamin therapy in children derives from the work of Cott. His reports cover several disorders ranging from juvenile schizophrenia to learning disabilities, but because no experimental data are presented, analysis of results is not possible. Cott also introduced the concept that orthomolecular mineral therapy and special diets for hypoglycemia might be used to treat behavioral abnormalities.

As with the Feingold diet, studies have provided no clear evidence that megavitamin therapy is of use in the treatment of developmental disabilities. Although vitamins are "natural," the doses are not. Vitamins can produce severe side effects, and the risk of toxicity of large doses of some vitamins taken for long periods is unknown. Until more convincing data can be obtained, this mode of therapy should not be encouraged.

Orthomolecular mineral therapy. The use of mineral supplements in treating developmental and learning problems has been made possible, at least partially, by the availability of accurate methods for measuring these substances in biological tissues and the easy access of one such tissue, hair. Problems lie not in the analytical method but in the usefulness of hair as a diagnostic tool and in the meaning of the results.

Hair analysis is complicated by long-term exposure of hair to the environment, the uncertainty of methods of removing environmental substances, the presence of minerals in some shampoos, the effect of organic solvents used to clean the hair, hair color, and the rate of hair growth. In addition, the norms for concentration of some elements vary with age, weight, and height. These factors usually are not taken into account when standards are defined.

Finally, a single value that falls below the range determined for an apparently normal individual does not in itself indicate a deficiency state. Other factors (eg, physiologic, nutritional) must also be determined. For example, mild zinc deficiency is associated with a normal plasma zinc level but a decreased hair zinc concentration. In severe zinc deficiency, the plasma zinc level is decreased, but hair zinc concentration may be normal.

There is little evidence to support an abnormal level of minerals in children with learning disabilities or to justify giving supplementary minerals in treatment. Because of the possible occurrence of positive balance for some of these substances and the risk of long-range damage caused by increased tissue concentrations of minerals, their use cannot be recommended at this time.

Hypoglycemia diets. Two conceptions are widely held concerning the role of sugar in behavior and learning problems. Some observers, who posit a rebound hypoglycemia, recommend frequent feedings with diets low in free carbohydrate and high in protein. Others are convinced that the intake of sugar leads to an immediate increase in hyperactive behavior; this belief does not appear to relate to any specific hypothesis.

The diagnosis of hypoglycemia usually is based on results of a five-hour glucose tolerance test. Problems frequently found with this test are inadequate dietary preparation of the subject, an incorrect glucose load, and a misunderstanding of norms for blood sugar concentration. The diagnosis depends on demonstration of a temporal relationship between the behavioral changes and a documented low blood sugar. This is rarely obtained.

Once again, these hypotheses have no supporting data. A diet low in sugar is good for dental health, but there is no basis on which strong recommendations can be made for dietary manipulation of sugar intake to treat behavioral symptoms.

Other therapies. New therapies are introduced almost daily for the treatment of behavior and learning problems. Many do not capture the imagination of the public, and others disappear following a brief period of popularity. However, several have managed to remain popular over many years, despite their controversial nature.

(1) Patterning. A patterning technique, used for neurologically handicapped children and for the treatment of reading problems, purportedly remediates abnormalities in neurologic organization by the imposition of passive patterns on the patient. There is no sound theoretical basis for this approach, and analysis of the studies available does not support the treatment's usefulness.

(2) Optometric training. This approach is based on the assumption that learning disabilities are due to abnormal visual perception and abnormalities in the coordination of eye movements and binocular fixation. Treatment involves a program of exercises to improve the abnormal functions. No controlled studies have been reported in peer reviewed medical journals to support this approach. Moreover, the technique attempts to provide a uniform etiology and treatment for a broad scope of learning disabilities, a view not consistent with findings based on modern neuropsychological research. It is now obvious that dyslexia in children may involve a large range of disabilities, most of which are unrelated to visual perceptual function.

(3) Vestibular stimulation. The technique of providing vestibular stimulation to the child by spinning or rocking is claimed by its proponents to improve sensory motor integration as well as several other rather global neurologic functions. As with many other techniques, this is claimed to be useful with a broad but poorly

defined range of cognitive and behavioral abnormalities. Studies to prove effectiveness are lacking.

Adverse effects of controversial therapies. Several of these therapeutic techniques, especially the orthomolecular therapies, raise concern about long-term biological complications due to unsuspected toxicity. Some of the others appear to be harmless, and there is a great temptation to go along with the parents' demands if they desire a therapeutic trial. But before such a course is embarked upon, a few considerations must be evaluated.

The first question is whether the new treatment will divert the child from more traditional and better documented methods of therapy. For example, parents who become involved with any of the nutritional approaches often want to eliminate all drugs from the child's regimen. If these include such agents as anticonvulsants, the problem becomes obvious.

Parents will find that the controversial therapies can be expensive, either because of the need for frequent treatments or the high cost of dietary supplements and organically grown, additive-free foods. Also, a major time commitment usually is necessary.

These therapies also may negatively affect the child. Children with learning disabilities generally have a poor self image and do not interact easily with peers. Dietary restrictions further set the child apart as being different and interfere with his or her ability to socialize with friends.

Family stresses may be caused by issues surrounding special diets, since it is virtually impossible to institute major dietary revisions without changing the eating habits of the entire family. Other members may object to these limitations and focus their hostility on the patient. They also may begrudge the time it takes to perform some methods of treatment.

Potential for harm must be considered for any treatment, no matter how innocuous it may seem. The medical literature is filled with “standard” techniques that many years later proved to be harmful. Use of oxygen in the treatment of premature infants is one example of the hazard of using a “natural” substance in an excessive dose.

Recommendations. When a patient asks for an opinion about a controversial therapy, the physician has an obligation to discuss the existing state of knowledge but is not required to actively participate in use of the therapy. Passive acquiescence with some of the least harmful (eg, additive-free diet) therapies is a compromise made by many practitioners. It is in the patient’s best interest, however, to insist on discussing associated problems that may arise from the use of even such simple measures.

As new treatment strategies are introduced, the following questions should always be asked: (1) Is the theory consistent with modern scientific knowledge? (2) Are claims for its usefulness broad or highly specific? (3) What is the potential for biological harm? (4) What are the hidden time, financial, psychological, and intrafamilial costs? and (5) Based on the above, what is the final risk-benefit analysis?

Understanding of the psychosocial aspects of patient care is most important, as is recognition of the needs of the family attempting to cope with a child who has a chronic disability. Above all, however, treatment must be scientifically based, and all therapies should be critically analyzed to define both their efficacy and potential for harm.

CHAPTER SIX

Other Service Needs

Research and experience have shown that the stimulation and encouragement provided by family living are beneficial to mentally retarded persons and help them realize more of their potential. Thus, current social policy favors retention of retarded individuals in their own homes or in home-like community settings whenever possible. This policy has led to the development of ancillary programs that enhance the care of mentally retarded persons. Such programs are concerned with mental health and social services, living arrangements, education, and prevocational and vocational training (see Table 9). The physician should be prepared to counsel mentally retarded patients and their families on how to obtain these services and gain access to appropriate facilities.

Mental Health and Social Services

The stress of caring for a mentally retarded child may produce a home atmosphere unfavorable for further individual progress or family integration. Parents who cannot secure adequate mental health and social services may be unable to resolve their own emotional problems and may stunt the emotional growth of their mentally retarded child through rejection or overprotection, impair the child's potential for maturation, and impede the development of siblings. Severe retardation may preclude a warm parent-child relationship.

Organized mental health and social services, with their interdisciplinary staffs, offer a variety of insights into individual problems and can be of value to the physician concerning management and counseling of both patient and family. Teachers, psychologists, speech and language therapists, and social workers frequently work with physicians in the diagnosis and care of mentally retarded children. In some cases, public welfare and family service workers also have intermittent or continuing contact with the child and family.

Table 9
Possible Components Of A Service System For Children's Mental Health Needs*

Diagnostic Needs	Treatment Needs	Educational Needs	Socialization Needs	Transportation Needs	Housing Needs	Advocacy Needs
Medical: Pediatric Internal Med. Neurologic Ophthalmologic ENT Psychiatric	Medical and dental treatment: General health Hospital Specialty clinics Psychiatric Neuromotor and sensory integration and rehabilitation	Generic programs Head Start Day Care	Preschool or day care	Training to use existing system	At home with natural parents	Individual
Psychological testing: IQ, perceptual-motor, projective tests		Specialty programs for speech, vision, hearing impaired, emotionally disturbed, mentally retarded	After-school programs	Access to special systems	Foster care	Group (such as National Association for Retarded Citizens, National Society for Autistic Children, the Candlelighters, and other self-help groups)
Social services			Respite care		Group residence	Community education
Educational evcluation			Support groups for parents and children		Residential facilities in the community	
Speech and audiologic			Recreational services		State institutions	
Laboratory: routine lab, x-ray/CAT scans, EEG, EMG			Spiritual care			

*The services listed here are available in most communities, although sometimes under different names.

When a child presents unusual, complex, or chronic physical and mental health problems, a social worker often is directly involved. Not only are social workers skilled in collecting information helpful in the accurate diagnosis of problems; they are expert in guiding parents and physicians through the confusing maze of educational and social services to find the precise help a particular child needs. The mental health system also relies heavily on social workers to provide direct treatment services in inpatient settings, child guidance clinics, community mental health agencies, and residential treatment centers. Clinical social workers may be involved in service delivery at all levels of the educational system, from early intervention programs that offer counseling services to parents of infants through upper grade programs in general and special education.

Needed services can be obtained by referring families to appropriate mental health/mental retardation agencies (these may be called developmental disability agencies), social welfare agencies, hospitals, and private practitioners. Physicians in small communities or rural locations often can devise alternatives to the complex services offered in metropolitan areas. In some cases, the components of a clinic can be put together: the local hospital and nursing service can be utilized and patients referred to accessible specialists, with the treating physician coordinating the services.

Living Arrangements

Across the nation, major efforts have been made to reduce the number of persons cared for in state institutions. Even for substantially impaired individuals, there is a growing variety of placement options, including family home care, skilled-care nursing homes, and convalescent hospitals. The current consensus is that smaller facilities are preferable, although no consistent relationship between facility size and quality of care has been demonstrated. Some very small family-style homes are more restrictive than larger boarding care settings in the same geographic region. There is no generally accepted standard for community residential programs, such as foster homes, group homes, and board and care homes. Staffing patterns vary greatly, as does the quality of care.

The location of facilities and community support services also are significant factors. As a general rule, urban settings provide a greater number of specialized services and opportunities for recreational activities than do rural areas.

Selecting an alternative arrangement. Placement immediately following the birth of even the most severely retarded child rarely is indicated, and no type of mental retardation is, in itself, an indication for residential care. Generally, it is best for the mentally retarded person to remain at home or in the community as long as that environment can meet his or her needs. If these needs cannot be met adequately, respite care in the form of home care services several times a week or temporary placement for a short time in an alternative setting may enable the family to keep the child at home. However, the time may come, usually after parents have contributed significantly to a retarded child's development, when parental and community resources--no matter how conscientiously applied--appear inadequate, and further progress requires the availability of specialized professional skills. When this occurs, it generally is necessary to explore the possibility of other living arrangements.

Discussing an alternative living arrangement for a retarded child is an agonizing experience for a parent. Therefore, premature introduction of the subject may cause the parents either to panic or become openly hostile. Proper timing is critical. Probably from the beginning of their awareness that their child is mentally retarded, parents will think about the possibility of placement and raise the question with the physician if given an opportunity. A great degree of emotional stress surrounds the need to resolve this question, and parents may interpret any mention of out-of-home care as a recommendation. However, after an adequate period in which they have had an opportunity to work through their feelings and do everything possible for their child at home, they may be prepared to view placement as an option.

Visiting various types of residences and becoming familiar with their staffs and programs enables the physician to keep abreast of the changing nature of alternative living arrangements and the newer kinds of residential care available. Rather than make a decision for the parents regarding placement of their child, he or she should sympathetically support their decision-making process and help guide them by presenting the widest possible variety of alternatives. Parents should understand that placement does not mean complete separation; they should be told about family visits, vacations at home, and the possibility of the child's eventual return.

In certain cases, the physician may want to point out the option of foster care in the community. To some parents, however, foster care may imply a negative judgment of their parenting abilities. They may feel that if they are unable to care for their child, no substitute parent can do so. In such cases, a more formalized residence for care should be advised.

To parents beset by intense feelings of guilt, care of their mentally retarded child outside the home may symbolize abandonment. In such cases, the parents may remain determined to keep the child at home, whether or not that choice seems wise to an outside observer. It may be necessary for more time to pass before the physician can determine whether the parents' decision was a good one.

Individual factors. Skilled nursing care may be necessary for severely retarded patients who require a degree of physical care that their parents or the community is unable to provide. These individuals usually are not ambulatory and may be neurologically impaired as well as mentally retarded.

Temporary out-of-home placement may be advantageous for patients who require the services of various specialists because of major medical problems. These include chronic illnesses, intractable seizures, and metabolic disorders as well as proneness to acute episodes, such as recurrent pneumonia. Other patients who may benefit from such placement are those who require special nursing services because they need certain types of medication or have feeding problems, recurrent seizures, intermittent illnesses, or deformities or other physical handicaps.

Alternatives to home care may benefit some children whose behavior renders their integration into the family or social structure difficult. Such children may be extremely hyperactive and seemingly unmanageable or severely withdrawn and uncommunicative. Other children may need special educational or vocational training that requires temporary placement.

The need for alternative care may become more apparent as certain problems in the child are noted. For example, in the youth or adolescent with mild retardation, problems in social adaptation may influence the decision. The daily care needs of severely or profoundly retarded children, particularly those with major physical handicaps that limit mobility or require constant nursing care, may eventually become unmanageable even for the ablest parent.

A knowledge of the family and its interactions is essential if the physician is to guide parents appropriately. Relationships between the retarded child and normal siblings are less critical than those between the child and parents. Even when the physician has such knowledge, the effects of decisions regarding the child often are unpredictable. For example, removal of a mentally retarded child from the home may actually worsen the family's difficulties, even though it benefits the child.

When out-of-home placement does occur, the physician should, if possible, remain in contact with the patient, his or her custodian, and the family.

Education

Until 1975, more than a million children with serious handicaps were excluded from American public school systems. Today, most of the four million handicapped American children are in school, and most receive instruction considered appropriate to their needs. This dramatic change resulted from the enactment of Public Law 94-142 (the Education for All Handicapped Children Act), which was passed in response to a growing recognition by the courts and society of the rights of handicapped children and the accompanying costs of providing the services those children needed.

Specifically, P.L.94-142 requires that free appropriate public education be made available to all handicapped children from 3 to 21 years of age, regardless of the severity of their handicaps or their families' ability to pay for services. The law mandates each public school system to:

- Locate, identify, and evaluate every handicapped child within its jurisdiction.
- Place the child in the least restrictive environment consistent with his or her special needs.
- Provide an individualized program of instruction designed to meet those needs.
- Arrange for related or supportive services necessary for the child to benefit from the individualized instruction program.

P.L.94-142 covers all children who require special education and related services, including those who are mentally retarded, hard of hearing, deaf, speech impaired, visually handicapped, seriously emotionally disturbed, orthopedically impaired, other health impaired, or multihandicapped, as well as children with specific learning disabilities. In addition, it mandates schools to be concerned with anything that might interfere with a child's educability, including medical and social problems.

The range of services required by the law includes early identification and assessment of disabilities, assistance by specially trained teachers and aides, speech and language therapy, special materials and equipment, counseling, psychological services, school health services, medical services for diagnostic purposes, physical and occupational therapy, special transportation to school, vocational education, and parental counseling. The selection of services provided at the local level depends on the needs identified for each child and funds available under federal and state programs.

All children identified as having handicaps must undergo assessment by an evaluation team. The parent or guardian must consent to assessment of the child and has the right to participate in and to appeal the results of the evaluation. Assessments must be made by qualified professionals, following regulations that call for procedures to be adjusted for specific deficits in health, hearing, or vision and to accommodate differences in background, culture, or language. Although the law does not specify the professional disciplines to be represented on such a team, physicians often are invited to participate.

P.L.94-142 requires that an annual education plan be developed for every handicapped child. Using information secured by the evaluation team, a child study team drafts an individualized education plan containing annual goals and short-term objectives for the child's education and identifies any related services that should be made available to the child.

The physician, often the first professional to recognize a child's handicap, may help to obtain benefits for such a child under P.L.94-142 by referring the parents to the director of special education or the superintendent's office in the local public school district. The extent of physician involvement in this process varies among physicians and school districts. Some physicians establish a working relationship with a person in the educational system, such as a special education coordinator or school psychologist, to whom they communicate their findings and suggestions for remediation. This kind of open communication leads to increased understanding of a given child's problems by both the physician and the educator.

Day care. Many young children, including handicapped children, attend day care centers. Physicians can help assure that day care is a positive experience by counseling parents on the arrangements best suited to each child, helping them deal with any feelings of anxiety or guilt about day care, and supporting local public efforts to ensure high quality day care environments. Several organizations have published guidelines on choosing a day care facility. Physicians may wish to obtain copies of these booklets for their own use and for the parents of their young patients.

Head Start. Since 1965, this federally funded program has provided educational, health, and social services to economically disadvantaged children throughout the country. By offering an enriched learning experience in a group setting, Head Start helps preschool children master basic concepts and become motivated to learn, enhancing their performance in elementary school.

Individual programs vary. Some Head Start programs accept children as young as 3 months of age, while others work only with children older than 2, 3, or 4 years. In some programs, all children participate as a group in a classroom setting. In others, teachers visit the children at home. In still others, home visits are combined with daily group sessions for the children. Some programs are more highly structured than others and emphasize school readiness skills.

All Head Start programs have been successful in improving the learning skills and social adjustment of the children involved. Researchers have found major differences between Head Start "alumni" and children from similar environments who have not attended Head Start programs. The Head Start children are less likely to be placed in special remedial classes when they enter elementary school and are less likely to be retained in a grade. They score significantly higher than controls on a fourth grade standardized mathematics test and also tend to score higher in reading.

Public Law 93-644 requires that at least 10% of the Head Start enrollment in each state be reserved for handicapped children (defined in the law as children who are mentally retarded, hearing or speech impaired, deaf, visually handicapped, seriously emotionally disturbed, orthopedically impaired, or learning disabled).

Some primary care physicians are involved with Head Start programs on a diagnostic and therapeutic level, while others are program consultants and advisors. Each local Head Start program has a health coordinator who serves as liaison between physicians and program staff. A physician who believes that a young retarded patient is eligible for Head Start should contact the local Head Start health coordinator.

Family needs. Families of mentally retarded children also have needs. All states are required to include due process safeguards to protect parents' rights and minimize the time lag that often has discouraged parents or guardians who have contested educational issues. Psychosocial supports may be available through community mental health centers, public welfare agencies, and community associations for retarded citizens (ARCs).

Prevocational and Vocational Training

Before they leave school, many mildly mentally retarded adolescents can be prepared for employment through prevocational counseling and evaluation, job placement assistance, and post-placement counseling. Some schools offer vocational training and operate cooperative programs that involve the school, vocational rehabilitation agencies, sheltered workshops, and outside employers.

The range of vocational possibilities for mildly retarded persons includes on-the-job training in industrial settings, specially designed occupational training centers, and closely supervised work experience. Aptitude and performance testing, counseling, and selective placement enhance the possibility of successful employment. Physical rehabilitation programs improve employability for some.

Educational services for mentally retarded children are the beginning of prevocational services. In order to work, a mentally retarded individual must have certain levels of ability with regard to communication skills, motor skills, and social skills.

Communication skills. Speech or language problems may be the most common of all disabilities affecting mentally retarded persons. Identification of the level of retardation provides guidelines for the types of services that are most likely to be effective, determination of the age at which progress may be expected, and reasonable long-term goals.

The degree of speech and language delay or disability in mentally retarded individuals is related to the degree of retardation. Most severely retarded and all profoundly retarded persons have significant language problems, and many develop only minimal communication skills, even as adults.

Recent developments in the area of communication have resulted in an improved outlook for retarded individuals in communicating with care providers and peers. One such approach is the use of communication boards that contain symbols or pictures representing objects or events of daily life. Others are electronic devices or modified typewriters and computers that can be manipulated with minimal use of muscles.

Mildly to moderately mentally retarded persons are likely to be able to develop useful communication skills and learn to speak in at least a limited way. Special education classes and teachers may help some of these individuals to further develop their communication skills.

Motor skills. Impairment of motor skills is not necessarily concomitant with mental retardation. Many of the same kinds of treatment and training are needed for nonretarded and retarded persons to develop gross motor skills (often under the supervision of an occupational therapist). The degree of retardation will give the physician some indication of the patient's potential to develop motor skills that will prepare him or her for possible employment.

Social skills. Many community programs, residential facilities, and certain other programs now include specialists who help mentally retarded individuals to develop interpersonal skills, participate in group social activities, and learn how to utilize leisure time. Individualized training may be required for some of these persons to acquire or maintain certain basic social skills or to reduce inappropriate social behavior.

These activities aid mentally retarded individuals in developing a sense of self-worth. In addition, the skills they learn may be transferable to subsequent sheltered workshop situations.

Included in the category of prevocational training activities are arts and crafts, music instruction and therapy, and religious instruction.

Some mentally retarded individuals can be trained for competitive employment, while others are able to function in sheltered workshops. These are becoming better known as a possibility for mentally retarded persons to perform work under contract. In various communities, tasks performed in sheltered workshops range from stuffing and sealing envelopes to handicraft work. Some moderately retarded adults can perform simple production tasks, compensating by diligence and perseverance for their lack of speed. Their level of intelligence, however, may not permit them to live independently. Sheltered work settings, combined with recreational and counseling facilities as well as group homes, may enable these individuals to live happily and productively in the community.

In addition to providing medical care, the physician helps mentally retarded patients and their families to become good "case managers" by facilitating their access to the community service needs described above. These areas are reviewed by the physician with patient and family during routine medical visits to be sure that changing needs are met as the retarded individual grows and develops.

CHAPTER SEVEN

Economic and Legal Considerations

Counseling mentally retarded patients and their families involves decisions that have significant economic implications. To competently guide these individuals and establish necessary linkages with community support systems, physicians must have a working knowledge of federal and state entitlements and local resources.

In addition, major changes in the legal rights of mentally retarded persons have occurred in the past 20 years. One of the most notable changes involves consent of the retarded individual regarding personal matters. Physicians should have current knowledge of these changes to effectively counsel mentally retarded patients and their families.

Accessing the Service System

The various service needs of mentally retarded children are addressed by a somewhat confusing array of agencies. For example, it is possible for a given child to undergo as many as six individualized evaluations with different teams in order to obtain services under Public Law 94-142: the Early and Periodic Screening, Diagnostic, and Treatment program; the Developmental Disabilities Act; Titles 19 and 20 of the Social Security Act; Crippled Children's Services; and the Disabled Children's program under Supplemental Security Income. Each program has its own target population, funding, regulations, and operational base. No single agency performs a central organizing function. The physician can assist parents of mentally retarded children in developing sufficient expertise to access the appropriate agencies and programs.

Medicaid and EPSDT

The Medicaid program was created by Congress in 1965 to provide financial support for health care services to the poor and severely handicapped. In some cases, this entitlement may be of interest to physicians. Among the basic requirements of the legislation are mandated payments for services delivered to the "categorically needy" (all persons receiving public assistance under Aid to Families with Dependent Children and most receiving assistance under Social Security Income for the aged, blind, and disabled) and the "medically needy" (individuals whose family income exceeds eligibility standards for the categorically needy but who are unable to pay part or all of their medical expenses).

Services covered under the Medicaid program include physician, hospital, laboratory, and x-ray services; family planning services; and early and periodic screening, diagnostic, and treatment (EPSDT) services for persons under age 21. While Medicaid usually reimburses providers for services delivered, EPSDT regulations require states to provide or purchase certain services for eligible children, including vision, hearing, and dental care; community outreach; case management; and transportation.

Entitlements Under the Social Security Act

Under Title 20, each state designs its own social services program. States set their program priorities after identifying the unmet needs of local communities. Local governments, interested organizations, and concerned citizens help decide what services should be offered, which persons should receive them, and how funds should be allocated to provide those services within the state. While states are given considerable discretion, Title 20 has certain federal requirements. For example, the services offered must be directed at one or more goals for individuals or families, such as financial self-support; self-sufficiency; protection of children and vulnerable adults from abuse, neglect, or exploitation; strengthening of the family; avoidance of inappropriate institutionalization by providing services in the local community; and appropriate institutional placement and services.

Federal grants are made to the states under Title 20 to finance services for persons in certain categories. Recipients of Aid to Families with Dependent Children (AFDC) are those whose needs are not met elsewhere. The aged, blind, and disabled are recipients of Supplemental Security Income under Title 16 or state supplemental payments. Services also can be provided to others whose incomes meet certain limits set by the states under the Income Eligible program. A subgroup of the Income Eligible Medicaid population also is eligible for medical assistance under Title 19. For this population, states may offer three classes of service without consideration of income: information and referral; family planning; and services for the purpose of protecting children or adults from abuse, neglect, or exploitation. Persons who receive such services without an income means test are classified in the "Without Regard to Income" category.

Vocational Rehabilitation Act

For older patients, physicians and parents will want to become familiar with the provisions of Section 504 of Public Law 93-112 (Vocational Rehabilitation Act), which is a civil rights provision mandating that there be no discrimination in providing vocational rehabilitation services under the act.

Reimbursement Issues

Third-party reimbursement for combined services (social, special education, psychological, and even recreational) generally is not difficult to obtain when mentally retarded patients are cared for in a medically directed inpatient setting. It becomes more problematic when treatment is given on an outpatient basis. Few public or private health insurance plans reflect the reality that at least half of all mental health interventions for children are made on an outpatient basis by persons other than trained mental health professionals.

Because the issues of reimbursement are complex, the physician has additional responsibilities when caring for a mentally retarded patient.

These responsibilities can be eased if the physician learns the system, works out unit costs, develops a treatment plan, communicates with the patient's family, and determines which responsibilities are primarily the physician's and which can be shared.

Costs Versus Benefits

In dealing with mentally retarded patients, simple measurements of cost versus benefit are sometimes unrealistic. On the one hand, it is almost always impossible to justify the cost of treating a mentally retarded child on the basis of anticipated outcome of care. On the other hand, it is not acceptable to turn away and say that nothing can be done for such a child; most such children can be helped.

The intellectual, emotional, and economic costs of long-term care can be appreciable. Judicious use of resources and cooperation among professionals will enhance the benefits and reduce the overall costs of such care.

Labeling

A child's problem must be diagnosed and labeled before he or she qualifies for federal entitlements. Physicians frequently are caught up in conflicting demands as they engage in this process. On the one hand, government programs require that a child be designated "mentally retarded," "learning disabled," emotionally disturbed," etc., before that child can become eligible for program services. On the other hand, some diagnoses can lead to entrenchment of undesirable behaviors by reinforcing negative parental and societal expectations. Thus, diagnoses can be double-edged swords that allow a child to obtain needed services while covertly prolonging his or her problem. Consequently, diagnostic categories should be used only when they cannot be avoided without detriment to the well-being of child and family.

Legal Changes

In the past, mentally retarded persons legally were unable to engage in certain activities (eg, sexual relations, childbearing, birth control, adoption). Many states prohibited the marriage of persons identified as having certain mental deficiencies or mandated the sterilization of some institutionalized retarded individuals as a condition of release. Today, however, the law and society increasingly recognize the considerable decision-making skills of many mentally retarded persons and have granted them the legal right to control their own lives.

Sexual relations. Appropriate education in matters relating to sexual intercourse should be made available to mentally retarded adolescents at levels they can understand, regardless of their chronologic age. As they mature, additional information should be provided to give them a basis for decisions about engaging in sexual activities and to develop their ability to refuse consent when appropriate. Substitute consent for sexual relations does not exist; sexual intercourse without consent of the parties involved constitutes criminal rape.

Marriage. Mentally retarded individuals who have not been declared legally incompetent may decide to marry without special restrictions. However, premarital counseling and supportive services after marriage should be available to them. A legally incompetent retarded person also has the right to marry if he or she is capable of understanding what the marriage contract entails. In some states, the guardian of such an individual must consent to the marriage.

If a genetically transmitted condition is involved, the mentally retarded person should receive appropriate genetic counseling to ensure that he or she understands the condition.

Childbearing. The Supreme Court decisions regarding a pregnant woman's right to terminate a pregnancy during the first trimester should extend to a mentally retarded pregnant woman who is capable of giving consent. Since termination of pregnancy is both highly intrusive and irreversible, close examination of such consent must be made with particular attention to whether it is voluntary.

Sterilization. Involuntary sterilization without informed consent or judicial review is illegal. Courts now require careful scrutiny of any consent to sterilization given by retarded persons. Substitute consent may be permitted, but some courts have required even legally incompetent retarded individuals to personally consent to sterilization.

Birth control. Although birth control measures generally are reversible and are less intrusive than sterilization, they should be provided only after adequate information has been given to the mentally retarded individual and his or her consent has been obtained. Such information must include an explanation of the risks of not employing birth control measures. If the retarded person cannot understand the procedure or its implications, substitute consent should be permitted only if the substitute consentor is independent (ie, has no personal interest in the outcome) and only when birth control measures have been found to be in the individual's best interest.

Some states permit minor children, under certain circumstances, to receive birth control information and services without parental consent. This right should be available to retarded minors who understand the nature and consequences of birth control.

Adoption. Adoption matters may involve the adoption or relinquishing of a mentally retarded child or the adoption or relinquishing of a child by mentally retarded parents.

Some states permit persons who adopt a very young child, and later discover that the child is mentally retarded, to terminate the adoption. In these instances, the adoption is treated as a voidable contract, with the adoptive parents empowered to void it by returning the child to adoption authorities.

Retarded persons who want to adopt a child must persuade a court to consider their petition. The court is likely to closely examine the potential adoptive parents' understanding of their responsibilities and to deny their petition unless they can demonstrate comprehension of those responsibilities.

Courts may transfer parental authority from natural to adoptive parents with consent of the natural parents, or without it if the court has found them unfit. When the natural parents are retarded, close attention must be paid to any consent they may give to relinquish their parental rights. If the court finds them unable or unwilling to consent to the adoption, it may proceed as an involuntary termination of parental rights, with the retarded parents represented by counsel.

Foster care. Foster parents generally can refuse to accept a mentally retarded child and can terminate a placement if they wish to do so. The foster child often has little authority to give or withdraw consent. However, most professionals respect the wishes of a retarded child who is able to give consent regarding his or her foster placement.

Custody following divorce. Some states grant children of a terminated marriage who are over a certain age the power to choose the parent with whom they will live. Mentally retarded children who fulfill the age requirement and who understand the nature of this decision should be accorded similar rights.

CHAPTER EIGHT

Prevention

Prevention of mental retardation can be characterized as primary, secondary, and tertiary. An example of primary prevention is the infant whose mother stopped drinking alcohol before she became pregnant. Identification of an infant with phenylketonuria (PKU) or congenital hypothyroidism and initiation of appropriate dietary treatment constitutes secondary prevention. In such cases, early treatment can prevent obvious manifestations of mental retardation but does not prevent the basic disorder. An example of tertiary prevention is identification of an infant with Down syndrome and initiation of early intervention techniques that may enhance the child's chances for a productive life. The greatest opportunities for prevention occur before conception and during pregnancy.

Some cases of mental retardation can be prevented with social measures and some with biomedical measures. Social measures are more difficult to implement, because they often are broad and encompassing and involve complex social policy. Yet, some preventive social measures are really "common sense" measures. For example, it is known that infants of mothers age 16 and under are at higher risk for handicaps and other problems. Also, women over age 40 are more likely than younger women to produce infants with Down Syndrome. If women in the high risk groups avoided pregnancy, some cases of mental retardation would be prevented. Additionally, if more mothers had better nutrition and avoided use of alcohol and drugs, fewer handicapped infants would be born.

Effects of Intrauterine Environment on Mental Retardation

Several maternal factors that are involved in creating an intrauterine environment for the fetus contribute to the possibility of mental retardation. These include but are not limited to age of the mother, maternal nutrition, prenatal care, socioeconomic group, and the mother's drinking and smoking habits.

In some cases, socioenvironmental and biomedical factors interact to cause mental retardation. Most notably, the risks are much higher for low-birth-weight premature infants than for normal infants. While prematurity sometimes has biological causes, including genetic defects, in certain population groups it is due to environmental factors and is seen more commonly in young teenagers. This age group statistically is more likely than others to have low-birth-weight premature infants. Some of these mothers lack proper nutrition and/or prenatal care during pregnancy.

Prematurity has been known to occur at a much higher incidence in poverty populations than in more economically advantaged groups.

Also, serious infections are much more common in populations that suffer from malnutrition, poor sanitation, and poor housing conditions.

Retardation associated with multiple factors may be prevented by efforts directed at all factors. A primary environmental strategy involves working with teenagers and members of certain socioeconomic groups to reduce the likelihood of pregnancy or, if it does occur, to encourage the pregnant woman to obtain appropriate prenatal care and nutrition.

Secondary and, perhaps, tertiary methods of preventing mental retardation involve biomedical approaches, such as the screening of newborns for metabolic disorders and the treatment of premature infants with intensive care in the perinatal period.

Effects of Maternal Use of Alcohol

During pregnancy, much of what the mother ingests crosses the placenta and affects the fetus. While alcohol is cleared from the adult system at the rate of 1 to 1-1/2 hours per drink, the same process requires up to 16 hours in the fetus. The human brain suffers dramatic and unexpected changes when the body absorbs large quantities of alcohol. Brain tissue may actually be destroyed.

In recent years, it has been discovered that alcohol abuse by pregnant women can lead to a variety of serious defects in their offspring, including facial deformities, central nervous system dysfunction, mental retardation, heart disorders, and skeletal problems or growth deficiencies. The characteristics and features that can affect children as a result of such prenatal alcohol consumption are known collectively as fetal alcohol syndrome (FAS).

FAS has three principal features: (1) *Central nervous dysfunction,* including microcephaly, poor coordination, and hypotonia; behavioral irritability in infancy; and attention deficit disorder in childhood. Mental retardation or delayed development has been an important finding in almost all clinical reports of FAS. (2) *Growth deficiency,* prenatal and postnatal deviations for length and weight. The growth deficiency typical of FAS is of prenatal onset, and postnatal catch-up growth is unusual. Some researchers report that, while heavy drinking during the first trimester probably has the greatest effect on fetal maldevelopment, excessive alcohol consumption in the later stages of pregnancy may have a greater effect on nutrition and size. Alcohol can deprive the body of nutrients necessary for normal fetal development, most notably zinc and magnesium. (3) *Facial characteristics,* including short palpebral fissures, low nasal bridge, epicanthic folds, short nose, indistinct philtrum, narrow upper lip, small chin, and flat midface. Drooping eyelids, crossed eyes, and minor joint and genital anomalies also are common.

The prognosis for more severely retarded children with FAS usually is poor, but most children who clearly have FAS function intellectually within the borderline to moderately retarded range, according to the standards of the American Association on Mental Deficiency.

In May 1983, the American Medical Association summarized its recommendations regarding fetal alcohol syndrome.

1. The evidence is clear that a woman who drinks heavily during pregnancy places her unborn child at substantial risk for fetal damage and physical and mental deficiencies in infancy...

2. The fetal risks involved in moderate or minimal alcohol consumption have not been established through research to date, nor has a safe level of maternal alcohol consumption...

3. Until such a determination is made, physicians should be explicit in reinforcing the concept that, with several aspects of the issue still in doubt, the safest course for a pregnant woman is abstinence.

Gestational Period and Mental Retardation

Several risk factors are associated with prematurity. Some studies indicate that 70% of premature infants who weigh less than 1,500 gm (3 lbs, 5 oz) at birth have various physical and mental disorders (eg, mental retardation, spastic diplegia, speech and hearing difficulties, visual disorders, behavioral problems). Although some controversy exists over the prevalence of these disorders in the premature group, prevention of prematurity has high priority in the prevention of mental retardation.

Premature infants may be more sensitive to the actions of oxygen and medications such as sulfonamide compounds and chloramphenicol. Also, because of the notably high frequency of physical and mental handicaps among the premature, growth and development evaluations should be performed regularly and often during infancy.

Infants with intrauterine-growth retardation have birth weights under 2,000 gm (4 lbs, 7 oz) and a gestation of 36 weeks or more. They are "low-birth-weight" infants born at term. Clinically, these infants may suffer extreme growth deficiencies and mental defects, although some are affected with only mild growth deficits and have a favorable prognosis for both mental and physical development.

A relationship may exist between postmaturity or dysmaturity and permanent neurologic sequelae. The postmature infant has a gestation of 42 weeks or longer, with more mature appearance and development that a term infant. Weight and length also may be greater. Early induction of labor, however, is not recommended. The dysmature infant usually has increased gestational age and shows evidence of wasting, respiratory distress, and neurologic signs; the risk of neonatal mortality is increased for these infants.

Maternal Metabolic Disorders

Several metabolic or endocrinologic disorders in the mother may affect the neonate. Infants born to mothers with diabetes mellitus have a higher-than-average risk of neonatal morbidity, congenital malformations, and mortality, and evidence suggests that neurologic sequelae may occur in some of these infants. However, diabetes can be assessed and controlled during pregnancy to minimize problems in the newborn.

Other maternal disorders that can affect the infant include myasthenia gravis, phenylketonuria, idiopathic thrombocytopenic purpura, and hypothyroidism. In a pregnant woman who has PKU, a modified diet with reduced phenylalanine intake decreases the risk of central nervous system deficits in the infant. Mental retardation can be prevented in neonates with PKU who are identified at birth and managed with appropriate dietary therapy, although the disorder cannot be cured.

The mother with hypothyroidism should be treated adequately during pregnancy. Protein-bound iodine (PBI) and butanol-extractable iodine (BEI) levels should be maintained within the normal range to encourage avoidance of congenital malformations and mental retardation.

Table 10
Effects of Drugs and Environmental Substances Upon The Fetus and Neonate Following Exposure in Utero

Maternal Drug Intake	Fetal or Neonatal Effects
(s) = suspected effects	
Antibiotics	
Aminoglycosides	8th nerve damage
Tetracyclines	Impaired bone growth; abnormal dentition and stained teeth
Sulfonamides	Kernicterus; anemia
Chloramphenicol	Death (gray syndrome)
Erythromycin	Liver damage
Nitrofurantoin	Hemolysis
Anticoagulants	
Warfarin (Coumadin)	Mental retardation; nasal hypoplasia with short limb dwarfism; a type of chondrodysplasia punctata; optic atrophy (s); hemorrhage; death (s)
Anticonvulsants	
Phenytoin	Mental retardation; facial dysmorphism; nail hypoplasia; (pre- and postnatal) growth retardation
Trimethadione	Mental retardation (s); facial dysmorphism; cardiovascular defects
Valproic acid	Spina bifida
Phenobarbital (excess)	Neonatal bleeding; death
Antidiabetics	
Tolbutamide	Thrombocytopenia
Chlorpropamide	Prolonged hypoglycemia
Insulin (shock)	Fetal death
Antimalarial Agents	
Primaquine	Hemolysis
Chloroquine (high doses)	Retinopathy; ototoxicity; death (s)
Antineoplastic agents	
Alkyating agents	Fetal death or wide variety of abnormalities
Aminopterin	Hydrocephalus; micrognathia; palate defects; low-set ears; hypotelorism; limb anomalies
CNS Agents	
Alcohol	Mental retardation; growth retardation; multiple anomalies; fetal alcohol syndrome (FAS)
Lithium carbonate	Ebstein's anomaly of tricuspid valve (s); cyanosis; flaccidity
Nicotine	Premature birth; small size; perinatal loss
Chlordiazepoxide	Withdrawal syndrome
Benzodiazepines	Hypothermia; facial cleft (s)
Meprobamate	Retarded development

Table 10 (Cont.)

Maternal Drug Intake	Fetal or Neonatal Effects
CNS Agents (continued)	
Meperidine	Neonatal depression
Primidone	Withdrawal syndrome
Heroin, morphine, methadone	Withdrawal syndrome; neonatal death
Phenothiazines	Hyperbilirubinemia; depression; hypothermia
Hexamethonium bromide	Neonatal ileus
Magnesium sulfate	CNS depression and neuromuscular block
Anesthetics (general)	Neonatal depression
Drugs Acting on Reproductive System	
Diethylstilbestrol	Vaginal adenosis; vaginal adenocarcinoma (rare); uterine anomalies; epididymal anomalies in male fetus
Progestins, testosterone	Masculinization of female fetus; advanced bone age
Miscellaneous Agents	
Propranolol (beta blockers)	Hypoglycemia; bradycardia; respiratory depression
Methylmercury	Growth retardation; psychomotor retardation
Lead	Mental retardation
Ammonium chloride	Acidosis
Adrenocortical hormones	Adrenocortical suppression
Prednisolone	Acute fetal distress; fetal death
Prednisone	Low birth weight
Antithyroid drugs	Hypothyroidism
Methimazole	Scalp defect (s)
Barbiturates	Coagulation defects; withdrawal syndrome
Anesthetics (local)	Fetal bradycardia and depression
Reserpine	Nasal congestion; lethargy; respiratory depression; bradycardia
Cholinesterase inhibitors (pesticides)	Transient muscle weakness
Quinine	Thrombocytopenia
Thiazide diuretics	Thrombocytopenia; salt and water depletion; neonatal death
Vitamin K analogs, excess estrogens	Hyperbilirubinemia
Isotretinoin	Hydrocephalus; microtia; congenital heart disease
Salicylates (large amounts)	Bleeding
Solvents	Neonatal depression
Solvents (organic)	CNS defects; neural tube defect(s)

Medications and Treatments During Pregnancy

The reaction of a developing fetus to drugs may differ from that of children and adults. For this reason, the physician should discourage self-medication during pregnancy and should keep all medication to an absolute minimum during the first trimester. While the majority of drugs do not lead to malformations in the fetus, unpredictable individual differences among patients have been noted. Table 10 summarizes the drugs that may have a teratogenic or cytotoxic effect on the fetus.

The use of nonprescription drugs during pregnancy also should be discouraged. For example, aspirin may adversely affect blood clotting in the neonate, while multivitamin preparations--taken in excessive quantities--can be harmful to the fetus. Although pregnant women are routinely encouraged to limit weight gain, they should be advised to do so without the use of over-the-counter weight reduction drugs.

Therapeutic radiation to the uterus may damage the fetus during pregnancy. However, the low levels encountered with diagnostic x-rays carry small hazard. In addition, the amount of radiation can be reduced by the use of ultrasensitive film, image intensifiers, and other recently developed technologies.

Complications of Delivery

Complications during delivery can lead to birth defects. Bleeding and toxemia, often associated with premature birth, result in a significant number of children with cerebral palsy, epilepsy, and mental retardation. Minor degrees of cerebral damage, including behavioral and specific learning disabilities, occur even in normal term pregnancies. Postnatal neurologic sequelae sometimes are associated with mechanical injuries at birth, such as those resulting from cord prolapse, malpresentations, and mid- and high-forceps deliveries. However, prenatal and postnatal factors producing anoxia and fetal distress appear to be of greater significance.

Maternal Infections and Diseases

Because acute bacterial infections during the third trimester may induce premature labor, such infections should be treated promptly and aggressively. Although tuberculosis is rarely seen during pregnancy, when present it can be transmitted to the fetus and, therefore, must be diagnosed and treated early. If either mother or infant has active tuberculosis at the time of delivery, both should be treated.

The majority of infections that occur in pregnant women are viral. Any severe viral illness within the first trimester--particularly in the first eight weeks of pregnancy--may injure the fetus. In the last trimester, a severe viral infection may precipitate premature birth.

The rubella virus is teratogenic during the first trimester, even in the case of inapparent maternal infection. The rubella vaccine is recommended for use in all children but is contraindicated in women who might be pregnant.

No reliable evidence indicates that the influenza virus is teratogenic, although an influenza infection that occurs during the last trimester may lead to premature birth.

The viruses of poliomyelitis, measles, mumps, chickenpox, and herpes simplex have been teratogenic in some cases. Herpes simplex in the newborn is associated with high risk of mortality and can be transmitted from the mother during vaginal delivery. Therefore, a woman in whom herpes simplex has been diagnosed should be delivered by Cesarean section and her newborn isolated until the mother's infection is in remission.

Congenital syphilis sometimes contributes to mental retardation. A routine serologic study is mandatory during the prenatal period. Antisyphilitic therapy, even if initiated in the third trimester, will protect the infant against infection.

Table 11
Maternal Infections That May Be Associated With Fetal/Neonatal Disease or Central Nervous System Sequelae

Agent	Effects on Fetus or Neonate	Prevention	Possible Postnatal Manifestations/Sequelae
Syphilis	Spontaneous abortion; stillbirth; prematurity; congenital syphilis	Prenatal serology and treatment; neonatal VDRL should be followed until negative or stable at low titre	Dental changes with delayed treatment; keratitis despite treatment; progression of symptoms and death without treatment
Tuberculosis	*Congenital* — Born to mother with active genital TB, miliary TB, TB meningitis, other evidence of hematogenous spread during pregnancy	Treatment of mother	None if treated
	Neonatal — Acquired by exposure to persons with sputum positive TB (pulmonary cavity, TB pneumonia); TB meningitis and miliary TB are not contagious	Separation from mother with active pulmonary or renal disease;[1] INH prophylaxis	
Toxoplasmosis	Mild-severe: Uveitis; chorioretinitis; intracranial calcifications (may not show until 2-3 mos.); hepatosplenomegaly; jaundice; micro- or hydrocephaly; seizures; prematurity; rash	None (avoid undercooked meat), but maternal seropositivity is protective[2]	Spasticity; mental retardation; recurrent posterior uveitis; visual loss; seizures
Cytomegalovirus[3]	*Congenital* — Chorioretinitis; jaundice; hepatosplenomegaly; petechiae; rash; low birth weight; microcephaly; heart disease; hearing loss	None	Sensori-neural hearing loss; defective tooth structure; spasticity; seizures; mental retardation; growth retardation; viruria for years/persistent postnatal infection

Table 11 (Cont.)

Agent	Effects on Fetus or Neonate	Prevention	Possible Postnatal Manifestations/Sequelae
Cytmegalovirus (continued)	*Neonatal* — Pneumonitis; hepatitis; pallor; atypical lymphocytosis (may occur in up to 30% of premature infants who receive multiple blood transfusions; no symptoms until 5-6 weeks of age)[4]	Use CMV antibody-negative blood; avoid CMV banked human milk.	CMV mononucleosis syndrome; generalized CMV infection; disease may be self-limited without sequelae
Rubella[5]	Subclinical mild-severe: Petechiae; pneumonia; hepatosplenomegaly; bone lesions; congenital heart disease; cataracts; deafness; IUGR;* rash	1) Active immunization of childhood population 2) Serologic screening of pregnant women and vaccination of susceptibles at time of delivery	Sensori-neural hearing loss; virus excretion for up to 2 years/persistent postnatal infection
Chlamydia trachomatis	Ectopic pregnancy; possible prematurity; possible spontaneous abortion; inclusion conjunctivitis; pneumonia (3-19 weeks)	Prenatal diagnostic testing of high-risk women and treatment of infected women; neonate given erythromycin (0.5%) or tetracycline (1%) eye ointment prophylaxis (prevents conjunctivitis only)	Possible pulmonary sequelae from pneumonia
Neisseria gonorrhoeae	Ectopic pregnancy; possible septic abortion; possible prematurity; ophthalmia neonatorum; arthritis; septicemia; meningitis	Prenatal diagnostic culture (all women) and treatment of infected women; neonate given silver nitrate (1% solution), erythromycin (0.5% ointment), or tetracycline (1% ointment) eye prophylaxis (prevents conjunctivitis)	Compromised vision or blindness (if no prophylaxis)
Group B streptococci (S. agalactice)	Possible spontaneous abortion; possible stillbirth; possible prematurity; septicemia; pneumonia; meningitis	Investigational	Possible speech, hearing, and visual problems; psychomotor retardation; seizure disorders
Coccidioides immitis	Pneumonia, disseminated disease (4-6 weeks)	None if treated promptly with amphotericin B	None if treated early; death if untreated

*Intrauterine growth retardation

Table 11 (Cont.)

Agent	Effects on Fetus or Neonate	Prevention	Possible Postnatal Manifestations/Sequelae
Hepatitis B	Prematurity; IUGR; subclinical mild-severe hepatitis (delay of onset up to 2-3 mos.)	1) Hepatitis B immune globulin (0.5 cc IM) in delivery room or as soon as possible after birth in first 48 hrs., same dose repeated at 3 and 6 mos.[6] 2) Hepatitis B vaccine (0.5 cc IM) at 3, 4, and 9 mos. of age	Increased risk of hepatocellular carcinoma; persistent postnatal infection
Herpesvirus hominis[3]	Subclinical fulminating disease; vesicular skin lesions; keratoconjunctivitis; hepatosplenomegaly; jaundice; pneumonia; encephalitis; chorioretinitis; microcephaly; coagulopathy	1) C-section (in cases of active genital infection)[6] 2) Protect infant from contact with secretions in mother or father with active fever blisters until healed[6]	Psychomotor retardation; seizures; death (depending on severity of illness); persistent postnatal infection)
Enteroviruses (ECHO)	Diarrhea; rashes; aseptic meningitis; possible fetal death[7]	None	*Severe neurologic impairments:* Seizures; psycho-motor retardation; developmental delay in 16% *Possible impairments:* IQ 70-89; serious behavioral problems in 26%[8]
Coxsackie B	Fulminating disease; myocarditis; hyper- and hypothermia; hepatitis; aseptic meningitis; fetal malformations[9]	None	Neonatal mental retardation; seizures; spasticity (rare)[10]
Rotaviruses	Diarrhea	Investigational vaccine	None
Varicella-zoster	Congenital varicella-zoster limb hypoplasia; eye malformations; cutaneous scars[11]	*Varicella:* If mother has onset of rash 5 days before to 48 hrs. after delivery, infant should receive Varicella-Zoster Immune Globulin (VZIG)[12] *Zoster:* None	None (if no malformations)

Table 11 (Cont.)

Agent	Effects on Fetus or Neonate	Prevention	Possible Postnatal Manifestations/Sequelae
Myxo- and paramyxovirus measles	Spontaneous abortion; low birth weight (IUGR)	Active immunization prior to pregnancy	Measles epidemics reported among college students
Mumps	Spontaneous abortion; endocardial fibroelastosis	Mumps immunization in mother prior to conception	
Arbovirus			
Western equine encephalitis	Congenital encephalitis (often fatal)	None	
HIV (AIDS/ARC)	Unclear (see column 4)	None	Opportunistic infections; lymphocytic intestitial pneumonitis; salivary gland enlargement; malignancies; microcephaly; neurologic abnormalities *Nonspecific features:* Lymphadenopathy; hepatomegaly; splenomegaly; failure to thrive; recurrent otitis media; thrush; diarrhea; nail clubbing *Immunologic abnormalities:* Marked IgG hypergammaglobulinemia; T_4 lymphopenia; T_4:T_8 reversal; depressed lymphoproliferative response; decreased thymulin plasma levels, suggesting deficient thymic secretory function[13]

[1]Smith MHD, Marquis JR: Turberculosis and other mycobacterial infections, in Feigin & Cherry (eds): *Textbook of Pediatric Infectious Disease.* Philadelphia, WB Saunders, 1981, pp. 1047-1048.
[2]Feldman HA: Toxoplasmosis, in Feigin & Cherry (eds): *Textbook of Pediatric Infectious Disease.* Philadelphia, WB Saunders, 1981, pp. 1047-1048.
[3]Overall, JC, Jr: Viral infections of the fetus and neonate, in Feigin & Cherry (eds): *Textbook of Pediatric Infectious Disease.* Philadelphia, WB Saunders, 1981, pp. 684-721.
[4]Ballard R, et al: Acquired cytomegalovirus infection in preterm infants. *Am J Dis Child* 133:482-485, 1979.
[5]No evidence of congenital malformation has been associated with vaccine strain of rubella.
[6]Corey L, et al: Genital herpes simplex virus infections. *Ann Intern Med* 98:958-972, 1983.
[7]Skeels MR, Ricker FM: Perinatal echovirus infection. *N Engl J Med* 305:1529, 1981.
[8]Sells CJ, et al: Sequelae of central nervous system enterovirus infections. *N Engl J Med* 293:1-4, 1975.
[9]Overall JC, Jr: Viral infections of the fetus and neonate, in Feigin & Cherry (eds): *Textbook of Pediatric Infectious Disease.* Philadelphia, WB Saunders, 1981, p. 711.
[10]Farmer K, et al: Follow-up study of 15 cases of neonatal meningoencephalitis due to Coxsackie virus B5. *J Pediatr* 87:568-571, 1975.
[11]Overall JC, Jr: Viral infections of the fetus and neonate, in Feigin & Cherry (eds): *Textbook of Pediatric Infectious Disease.* Philadelphia, WB Saunders, 1981, p. 713.
[12]CDC: Recommendation of the Immunization Practices Advisory Committee: Varicella-Zoster Immune Globulin — United States. *MMWR* 30:15-23, 1981.
[13]Rahwa S, et al: Spectrum of human T-cell lymphotropic virus type III infections in children: Recognition of symptomatic, asymptomatic, and seronegative patients. *JAMA* 255:2299-2305, 1986.

Acquired Immune Deficiency Syndrome (AIDS) and AIDS Related Complex (ARC) have been identified in neonates born to mothers who have AIDS, are members of certain groups at high risk for AIDS, or are sexual partners of members of high-risk groups. The route of transmission in these children is unknown; the retrovirus may be acquired in utero, from infective maternal blood at the time of delivery, or postnatally. Developmental and neurologic abnormalities have been observed in many of these infants.

Measles has been known to lead to abortion or stillbirth. Although widespread use of the live attenuated measles vaccine has greatly reduced the incidence of this disease, occasional outbreaks are reported in unvaccinated populations.

Cytomegalovirus infection, as well as toxoplasmosis (a protozoan infection), may be transmitted from an asymptomatic mother to the fetus. No therapy or preventive measures are known for these infections. Subsequent offspring are not affected.

Prenatal Diagnosis

Prenatal diagnosis encompasses several procedures, including ultrasonography and amniocentesis, that assess the condition of the fetus. Test results may provide information about certain conditions. If the fetus is found to be affected, the parents can be offered the option of terminating the pregnancy. Once a defect has been identified, the decision to interrupt the pregnancy will depend on the seriousness of the defect, the couple's attitude toward abortion, and their understanding of the affected infant's prognosis. Even when the physician believes that the parents will choose not to terminate a pregnancy if fetal defects are found, a prenatal diagnosis may better prepare them for the birth of an abnormal infant. Prenatal diagnosis of a few treatable conditions will allow institution of treatment immediately after birth.

Ultrasonography. An ultrasonogram involves passage of ultrasonic waves through the abdomen of the pregnant woman, providing an image of the uterus, fetus, and placenta. Ultrasonography can be used to determine (a) if the uterus contains more than one fetus, (b) the approximate gestational age of the fetus, and (c) the position of the placenta so that the obstetrician can avoid it if amniocentesis is to be performed. Ultrasonography also may detect such abnormalities as a small or large head or an open spinal defect.

Amniocentesis. Transabdominal amniocentesis is one of the most widely used methods of prenatal diagnosis. Because the fetus sheds epidermal cells and other substances into the surrounding amniotic fluid, withdrawal of a small amount of fluid and examination of these cells reveals certain chromosomal abnormalities and metabolic errors. The most frequent and best known chromosomal abnormality that produces mental retardation is trisomy for chromosome 21, resulting in Down syndrome. Several metabolic diseases that produce mental retardation also are detectable from cultured amniotic cells, including Tay-Sachs disease. Additionally, the increased concentration of alpha-fetoprotein in the amniotic fluid itself may indicate abnormalities in the fetus, such as an open spinal defect.

Amniocentesis ordinarily is performed in the 15th to 16th weeks of pregnancy, measured from the first day of the mother's last menstrual period. This procedure is widely accepted because of its high level of accuracy in diagnosis--more than 99%--and its low risk to mother and fetus. Spontaneous abortion is an uncommon complication.

The procedure involves insertion of a thin, hollow needle through the mother's abdominal wall and uterus, into the amniotic fluid sac. Approximately one ounce of fluid is withdrawn into a plastic syringe. Uncultured cells are tested for some conditions, and other cells are placed in culture for chromosomal studies and other biochemical tests.

Table 12
High-Risk Infants*

FAMILY HISTORY	
Presence of mutant genes	Previous defective sibling
Central nervous system disorders	Parental consanguinity
Low socioeconomic group	
PRECONCEPTIONAL MEDICAL HISTORY	
Irradiation	Cardiovascular or renal disease
Nutrition	Thyroid disease
Hypertension	
OBSTETRICAL FACTORS	
Maternal age <16 or >40	Size of infant
Elderly primipara; prolonged infertility	Fetal loss; perinatal death; stillbirth; premature delivery
Excessive parity	Miscarriage immediately preceding pregnancy
Age 30 with short inter-pregnancy interval	Pre-eclampsia; eclampsia
PRESENT PREGNANCY	
Unwanted pregnancy	Narcotic addiction
Diabetes mellitus	Medications (those known to be contraindicated)
Hypertensive cardiovascular disease	Pre-eclampsia; eclampsia
Hyperthyroidism under treatment	Multiple birth
Poor nutrition	Oligohydramnios
Pyuria; pyelonephritis	Rh isoimmunization with rising anti-Rh titre
Infectious disease: rubella, syphilis, tuberculosis, hepatitis, AIDS	Indication for cesarean section
Irradiation	
LABOR AND DELIVERY	
Absence of prenatal care	Abruptio placentae
Precipitate, prolonged, or complicated delivery	Hemorrhagic complications
Abnormal presentation or breech	Fetal heart aberrations
Prolonged rupture of membranes	Meconium staining
Low birth weight, especially <1500 grams; gestational prematurity; small for dates	Scalp blood pH 7.2 or lower
	Low Apgar score 1 minute, 5 minutes, and 10 minutes
PLACENTA	
Single umbilical artery	Placentitis
Massive infarction	Amnion Nodosum
NEONATAL	
Hyperbilirubinemia	Fever
Hypoglucosemia	Congenital defects
Apneic episodes	Severe hemolytic disease
Convulsions	Survival following meningitides, traumatic intracranial episodes
Sepsis	
Asphyxia	

*Based on table prepared by Sterling Garrard, M.D.

Fetal monitoring. In certain "high-risk" situations, either a maternal disorder or an abnormality within the fetus or newborn may produce neurologic sequelae (see Table 12). Fetal monitoring offers a valuable tool that encompasses the use of various biochemical and electrophysiologic sensors to detect fetal well-being during maternal labor. When used correctly, fetal monitoring techniques are practical and make possible improved observation of the fetus. All patients with increased risk factors, such as maternal illness or clinical signs of fetal distress, should be monitored.

Electrophysiologic continuous monitoring of the fetal heart rate may be obtained by placement of sensors on the maternal abdomen or directly against the fetal scalp in the birth canal. This technique permits observation of beat-to-beat changes in the fetal heart rate. To be most useful, the monitoring procedure must correlate fetal heart rate with maternal in utero pressure measurements (labor contractions). These contractions act almost as a "stress test" and provide earlier information about fetal distress than use of the heart rate as a single parameter.

According to a report of the American Medical Association Council on Scientific Affairs, "Continuous EFM is clearly warranted in high-risk pregnancies. Examples of high-risk pregnancy may include (1) antepartum risk indicators; (2) presence of meconium-stained amniotic fluid; (3) intrauterine growth retardation; (4) preterm or postterm gestation; (5) use of oxytocin in labor; and (6) abnormalities of fetal heart rate obtained by other methods."

The pressure sensors may be applied abdominally or transvaginally. Both for heart rate and in utero pressure, vaginal application of the sensors provides information that is clearer and therefore less confusing to interpret.

Prevention Through Mass Screening

Phenylketonuria, like Tay-Sachs disease, is caused by a single abnormal recessive gene; is manifested by deficiency of the enzyme, phenylalanine hydroxylase; and affects approximately 1 in 15,000 liveborn infants.

Diet is the major source of phenylalanine, one of the amino acids. It is necessary for normal growth and body functions, but in excessive amounts it can cause permanent brain damage. Phenylalanine is normally converted in the body cells to another amino acid, tyrosine. In PKU, the enzyme or a cofactor is deficient and phenylalanine is accumulated in the developing brain. Accumulation can be prevented by adherence to a diet very low in phenylalanine.

Infants are routinely screened at birth for PKU. If any doubt exists about the test results, the test should be repeated when the infant is several weeks to a month old.

In nearly all states, the screening test for phenylketonuria in newborns is mandatory. These and other, much rarer conditions that cause mental retardation can be detected in the neonate by testing a small specimen of blood, with a follow-up test performed later to verify the findings. Since the late 1960s, screening of newborn infants for PKU has become routine as a means of identifying infants so that dietary treatment can begin before brain damage occurs.

The test for PKU is fairly simple and should always be performed on an infant with an affected sibling or in whom the physician suspects a neurologic disorder. Vomiting, irritability, eczema, seizures, and a peculiar odor to the urine are frequent early signs of phenylketonuria, and the test should be performed in suspect infants. In mental retardation with no obvious etiology, it should be performed as part of the diagnostic assessment.

As in the case of PKU, neonatal screening for congenital hypothyroidism is mandatory in nearly every state. Thyroid hormone is necessary for growth, brain development, and other body functions. Congenital hypothyroidism occurs in one of approximately 5,000 births. Untreated, affected infants usually become severely mentally retarded and understatured. In an infant with congenital hypothyroidism, early identification will lead to thyroid replacement therapy before the onset of significant brain damage.

Phenylketonuria and congenital hypothyroidism are two examples of devastating conditions the effects of which can be prevented by fairly simple therapeutic measures.

Many rather rare genetic defects also lead to accumulations of incompletely metabolized compounds (eg, hypertriglyceridemia, homocystinuria, histidinemia, branched chain ketonuria, galactosemia, phytanic acid storage disease) and have responded, sometimes quite well, to dietary restrictions of the critical metabolic substrate. Although these conditions are rare, several states have mounted simple, inexpensive blood and/or urine screening tests that can detect several abnormalities in a single sample from an infant.

Other Observations in Newborns

Certain types of mental retardation can be prevented or averted by early initiation of treatment. Physicians should be alert for infants who do not "look right," are not thriving, are experiencing drug reactions, have parents with blood group incompatibilities, or have certain congenital anomalies or severe infections.

Failure to thrive. The physician should suspect galactosemia in any infant who fails to thrive. Cataracts, hepatomegaly, and jaundice may be present. Diagnosis can be made with a specific chemical test. Early treatment with a galactose-free diet has been successful in many cases.

The physician also should be alert to the onset of signs and symptoms of cretinism, such as lethargy, irritability, anemia, constipation, and retardation of growth. Prompt and aggressive therapy is necessary, as is continuous follow-up with determination of bone age, protein-bound iodine values, and growth.

Pharmacologic problems. The reaction of premature and full-term infants to drugs is different from that of children or adults. Table 10 summarizes the more important effects of frequently used drugs on the newborn.

Metabolic, hematologic, hormonal, or neurologic disturbances are common. Overdosage in the mother is the most frequent cause of toxicity. For example, vitamin K in therapeutic doses of 1 to 2 mg causes no damage, but amounts in excess of 50 mg may be toxic. Little is known about the processes of biochemical maturation in the brain of the fetus and neonate. The vulnerability of this system to the actions of certain drugs is established (eg, kernicterus, related to sulfonamide

Table 13
Evaluation of the Newborn Infant*

Sign	0	1	2
Heart rate	Absent	Below 100	Over 100
Respiratory effort	Absent	Slow, irregular	Good, crying
Muscle tone	Limp	Some flexion of extremities	Active motion
Response to catheter in nostril (tested after oropharynx is clear)	No response	Grimace	Cough or sneeze
Color	Blue, pale	Body pink, extremities blue	Completely pink

Sixty seconds after the complete birth of the infant (disregarding the cord and placenta), the five objective signs above are evaluated and each is given a score of 0, 1, or 2. A total score of 10 indicates an infant in the best possible condition.

*Modified from Virginia Apgar: "Current Research in Anesth. & Analg.," 32:260, 1953. Nelson, W: *Textbook of Pediatrics,* 9th edition, p. 357, 1969.

compounds). Less obvious neurologic sequelae may follow exposure to drugs that cause respiratory depression and cyanosis or those that may interfere with normal enzyme activity through competitive inhibition or alter the permeability of the blood-brain barrier. Any drug that lowers maternal blood pressure to hypotensive levels may potentially cause hypoxic damage to the fetus. A recording of the one-minute and five-minute Apgar scores can alert the physician to the presence of hypoxia or natal distress (see Table 13). Assessment of heart rate, color, muscle tone, respiratory rate, and cry will identify infants in immediate danger whose developmental status should be followed carefully.

Rh incompatibility. The problem of blood group incompatibility and its role in damage to the central nervous system has been virtually eradicated with the identification and immunization of mothers who have antibodies. It is important that mothers be screened during the prenatal period, so that possible blood group incompatibilities can be detected and treated early.

Hyperbilirubinemia in the premature infant demands special attention. A bilirubin level of 20 mg/100 cc or greater within the first 72 hours of life, or a rapidly rising level, indicates the need for an exchange transfusion. Multiple exchanges may be necessary to keep the level under 20 mg/100 cc.

Similarly, the problems of hyperbilirubinemia and erythroblastosis may be solved by newer measures aimed at prevention rather than treatment. These include use of ultraviolet light and injection of high titre Rh antibodies into the Rh-negative mother after the birth of her first Rh-positive baby.

Postnatal Surgery

The best example of postnatal surgery is the procedure for hydrocephalus. Early detection is necessary to prevent irreversible damage. Routine head measurements should be recorded for all infants during the first year of life. CAT scans allow accurate diagnosis of hydrocephalus. Increased frequency of neural deficits and other anomalies has been found in infants with one umbilical artery.

Infections: Meningitis and Encephalitis

Some infections are preventable or treatable; others are not. An infant who survives the acute crisis of meningitis or encephalitis should be watched carefully. Bacterial meningitis may be followed by permanent neurologic sequelae. Meningitis due to Hemophilus influenzae, in particular, may show such sequelae. Viral encephalitis and prolonged seizures during acute infections (eg, roseola) also have been reported.

Preventive measures include use, as appropriate, of measles vaccine; early recognition and prompt treatment of bacterial meningitis; and tuberculosis case-finding by routine tuberculin tests, especially among high-risk groups. Conversion of the tuberculin reaction at any time in childhood indicates the need for treatment.

Trauma, Accidents, and Poisons

Mental retardation due to head trauma from automobile accidents can be prevented. The use of restraining devices for infants and young children and automobile seat belts for older children are primary preventive measures and are mandated by law in some states.

Mental retardation due to lead poisoning is preventable. While the prevalence of lead poisoning has declined, some cases still occur, and body levels of lead that once were thought safe are no longer considered so.

In the past, the most common cause of lead poisoning in children was ingestion of flakes of lead-based paint used on the interiors and exteriors of older houses. As a result of eating the peeling paint, which has a sweet taste, children developed lead poisoning. Now environmental pollution, such as that caused by auto emissions and the manufacture of lead-based products, is a more significant source of lead poisoning.

With treatment, some patients recover completely from lead poisoning, but others are left with permanent brain damage. The problem affects adults as well as children, but its effects on children between ages 1 and 6 are most pronounced.

Two major strategies exist for preventing lead poisoning. One is to eliminate the hazard; the other is to screen at-risk individuals to determine whether they have higher than normal blood levels, indicating that they are in danger of lead poisoning. Steps then can be taken to prevent subsequent exposure.

Parents should be aware that it is dangerous for children to eat paint or play in areas with a high concentration of lead in the soil. Plant managers can use techniques such as air monitoring to determine the lead level in the air and detect an unacceptable build-up. They also can institute practices that reduce the amount of lead in the plant, such as isolating more hazardous operations from the general plant area and avoiding practices that create dust clouds.

Child Abuse*

Many children have suffered brain damage from head injuries associated with physical abuse. It is estimated that more than 125,000 new cases of physical child abuse occur annually in the United States. Physical child abuse is defined as the nonaccidental injury of a child, ranging from minor bruises and lacerations to severe neurologic trauma and death.

Nonaccidental trauma is the most easily identified type of child maltreatment and that most commonly seen by physicians.

*Adapted from *AMA Diagnostic and Treatment Guidelines Concerning Child Abuse and Neglect*, American Medical Association, 1985.

Characteristically, the child's injuries are more severe than those that could reasonably be attributed to the claimed cause.

Vulnerable families. The etiology of child abuse is an interactional one, and the primary care physician must take into account social, familial, and psychological as well as physical factors. While it may be impossible to predict accurately which individuals are at high risk as victims or perpetrators of child abuse, often it is possible to identify groups of individuals who are at greater risk. Correlations between child maltreatment and family characteristics that have been identified include the following:

- Child abuse is reported more frequently in low-income families. This may be due to underreporting among other socioeconomic groups; in fact, child abuse occurs in all social and economic strata.

- Socially isolated families (ie, those with no external support systems) tend to be more abusive.

- Violence toward children is especially common in families where husbands and wives resort to violence on one another.

- Individuals who are exposed to abnormal child rearing practices and who are maltreated as children appear to be more likely to become abusive parents.

- Parental expectations inconsistent with the child's developmental abilities often are observed in cases of maltreatment.

- Stressors such as alcohol and drug misuse, inadequate housing (eg, overcrowding), and mental illness are associated with maltreatment.

Vulnerable children. Characteristics that place children at increased risk of abuse include:

- premature birth;

- birth of a child to adolescent parents;

- colic, which renders an infant difficult to soothe;
- congenital deficiencies or abnormalities;
- hospitalization of the neonate who lacks parental contact;
- presence of any condition that interferes with parent-child bonding.

Diagnosis. The physician must conduct a complete physical examination, including developmental testing, on any child who may be a victim of abuse. During the diagnostic process, the physician should understand and assess the plausibility of historical and medical antecedents of the child's injury, determine the dimensions of continued risk to the child, and obtain the past medical history of the child and family members. Laboratory studies (eg, x-ray, CAT scan, coagulation studies, blood tests) are useful in delineating the nature and extent of current trauma and in defining the presence of previous trauma.

Reporting. Children who have been abused must be identified for their own protection. In all states, physicians who provide services for children are required by law to report suspected incidents of abuse. As mandated reporters, they are afforded legal immunity for such reports, and most jurisdictions may impose civil or criminal penalties for failure to report.

Other Causes of Mental Retardation

Physicians have observed that the occurrence of two or more febrile seizures may indicate a predisposition to later seizures. Further, prolonged seizures--particularly status epilepticus--with asphyxia may produce brain damage. Consultation with a neurologist may bc hclpful in instituting appropriate treatment.

Hypernatremia sometimes occurs in infants with diarrhea who are treated with skim milk or proprietary electrolyte solutions. Experimental and clinical data suggest that the elevated serum sodium may cause brain damage.

Genetic Counseling

Genetic counseling involves advising a family about the risk of occurrence of mental retardation and the problems that may arise from its occurrence. Indeed, identification of high-risk couples is one method of primary prevention of birth defects and mental retardation. Concerned potential parents can be advised of the medical facts regarding the severity and prognosis of the genetic disorder, the risk of its recurrence if they already have a retarded child, and options available for managing the affected child and for avoiding recurrence. Choices may depend on social, ethical, and religious issues as well as on the medical estimate of the disorder's burden on the affected family and individual.

Genetic counseling requires considerable training and sensitivity. It is often preferable to refer appropriate couples to specialized centers for this purpose.

In many cases, the need for counseling is recognized by the pediatrician, the obstetrician, or another primary care physician after the delivery of a defective child. Such an urgent and unexpected situation may arouse feelings of guilt, anxiety, or anger in both parents and physician. While counseling before pregnancy is preferred, and many advances in antenatal diagnosis are aimed at early detection, occasional unanticipated genetic defects appear after delivery. Unfortunately, some of these (eg, Huntington disease) cannot be recognized until mid-life.

In general, genetic counseling efforts are directed toward identifying individuals who may be at high risk of delivering an infant with a birth defect. Indications for referring a patient for genetic counseling include:

- family history of an inherited disorder;
- genetic or congenital anomaly in a family member;

- parent who is a known carrier of a chromosomal translocation;
- woman who has previously given birth to a child (children) with chromosomal aberrations;
- parent who is a known carrier of an autosomal recessive disorder in which *in utero* diagnosis is possible;
- abnormal somatic or behavioral development in a previous child;
- mental retardation of unknown etiology in a previous child;
- pregnancy in a woman over age 35;
- specific ethnic background that may suggest a high rate of genetic abnormality (eg, Tay-Sachs disease);
- three or more spontaneous abortions and/or early infant deaths; and
- infertility

Obtaining genetic counseling. Persons interested in receiving professional advice now have numerous resources. In recent years, the number of genetic counseling centers has increased rapidly. More than 200 major university-based centers, with many satellites, are now in operation.

Since the elimination of poliomyelitis as a public health problem, The March of Dimes has directed its efforts toward prevention of birth defects and improving the outcome of pregnancies. This organization also publishes an international directory of resources relevant to genetic disorders and can refer parents to appropriate genetic clinics.

Social and Environmental Considerations

All of a child's experiences, biological and social, affect his or her physical and mental growth and development. These experiences may be modified favorably or unfavorably by intrinsic factors, such as genetics, and extrinsic factors, such as environment. In considering possibilities for prevention of mental retardation, three basic aspects interact significantly. Etiologies that are environmental, those that stem from inadequate overall health care, and those based on the lack of nurturing are not independent factors. However, the area in which most changes are likely to occur is the third, with improvements in nurturing activities. Nurturing is closely related to socioeconomic level and relationship with parents and peers.

Functional Classification of Services

Functional Classifications	Organizations and Services
Prevention	Prenatal services; Planned Parenthood-World Population; American Eugenics Society; immunization services; public health nursing; screening programs (eg, PKU screening)
Detection and Diagnosis	Specialized mental retardation clinics; appropriate consultants, medical and nonmedical; school personnel; public health nursing
Treatment and Management	
1. Newborn	Visiting Nurse Assoc; public health nursing
2. Office	Public information pamphlets available from many sources
3. Well-baby clinics	Public health programs; Red Cross (Gray Ladies); Gems (Good Emergency Mother Substitutes) to furnish transportation and baby-sitting services
4. Hospitals and outpatient services	Specialized care (neurologic, psychiatric, etc.)

5. Medical rehabilitation (consulting services; special appliances)	American Speech and Hearing Assoc; National Society for Crippled Children; United Cerebral Palsy Assoc (UCPA); state services for crippled children; vocational rehabilitation; service organizations (Lions Club, Quota Club, Junior Chamber of Commerce, etc.)
6. Psychological evaluation	Public and private school systems; American Psychological Assoc; rehabilitation centers; outpatient clinics
7. Nursing services	Voluntary and governmental public health agencies
8. Social services	Patient: Public and private social agencies; church-related programs Community: Health-Welfare Council; Council of Social Agencies
9. Finances	Individual: Public assistance programs; private social agencies; national foundations Community: United Fund; service organizations; crippled-children's services
10. Counseling Psychiatric	Private practitioners; mental health clinics; child guidance clinics
Psychological	Private practitioners; mental health clinics; child guidance clinics; public schools
Pastoral	Ministerial associations; individual churches; clergymen

Genetic	University medical centers
Parental	Local chapters, National Assoc for Retarded Citizens (NARC); United Cerebral Palsy Assoc
11. Family planning	Planned Parenthood Assoc; family service agencies; clergy
12. Day care and foster care	Parent groups (NARC); social agencies (public and private)
13. Residential care	Designated agency for public institutions; American Assoc on Mental Deficiency; directory of public and private institutions
14. Postresidential care	
Half-way houses	Institutional social service referral
Foster care	Institutional social service referral; social welfare services

Educational Services

1. Preschool	Nursery school associations; board of education; parent groups; NARC; UCPA
2. Regular schools	Board of education; public, private, and church-related schools
School dropouts	Guidance counselors; mental health clinics
Vocational education	Work-study programs; guidance counselors

3. Special classes	
Educable, trainable	Board of education, special education division; parent-sponsored classes; NARC; UCPA
4. Schools for the handicapped	
Mentally retarded, multiply handicapped	See Porter-Sargent School Directory, Boston, MA
5. Parent-sponsored training classes	Local chapters, NARC and UCPA
6. Classes for adult retarded	Urgently needed
7. Parent education	NARC; UCPA; family service agencies; ministerial associations; public health services
8. Public education	Local news media; PTA; civic clubs; medical and lay journals; training films; medical speakers' bureau

Vocational Rehabilitation

1. Prevocational evaluation	State vocational rehabilitation agency
2. Vocational evaluation 3. Vocational counseling and guidance 4. Vocational training 5. Selective placement (regular employment; sheltered workshops; occupational day-care centers)	Local school systems; other private rehabilitation facilities and services, such as Good Will Industries; local trade schools

Recreation and Leisure-Time Activities

1. Local activities	YMCA; YWCA; boys' clubs; settlement houses
2. Summer camps	NARC; Easter Seal organizations; Kennedy Foundation; church groups
3. Social and cultural enrichment	4-H Clubs; Girl and Boy Scouts; field trips; church groups; fraternity and sorority activities; Big Sister/ Brother organizations

Other

1. The law and the retarded	Domestic relations courts; juvenile courts; probation officers; parent associations; NARC; guardianship planning; eugenics; bar associations; law schools
2. Education of the physician	Medical and specialty societies; meetings; journals; continuing education
3. Research	University hospitals and research centers; journals

4. Planning and coordination	State and local councils of social agencies; state departments with interest in retardation; NARC; National Assoc for Mental Health; responsible state agencies
5. Legislative and political support	NARC; League of Women Voters; Council of Governments; state legislative councils; county and city governments; school boards
6. Education of the clergy	Pastoral counseling; hospital chaplains; theological training

Physician Bibliography

Farmer TW (ed): *Pediatric Neurology (ed 3).* Philadelphia, J.B. Lippincott Company, 1982.

Green M: *Pediatric Diagnosis: Interpretation of Symptoms and Signs in Different Age Periods (ed 4).* Philadelphia, W.B. Saunders Company, 1986.

Grossman HJ (ed): *Classification in Mental Retardation.* Washington, American Association on Mental Deficiency, 1983.

MacMillan D: *Mental Retardation in School and Society (ed 2).* Waltham, MA, Little, Brown and Company, 1982.

Menkes J: *Textbook of Child Neurology (ed 3).* Philadelphia, Lea and Febiger, 1985.

Smith DW: *Recognizable Patterns of Human Malformation.* Philadelphia, W.B. Saunders Company, 1982.

Szymanski S, Tanguay PE: *Emotional Disorders of Mentally Retarded Persons: Assessment, Treatment, and Consultation.* Baltimore, University Park Press, 1980.

Volpe J: *Neurology of the Newborn (ed 2).* Philadelphia, W.B. Saunders Company, in press.

Zigler E, Hodapp RM: *Understanding Mental Retardation.* Cambridge University Press, 1986.

Resources for Parents

Listed below are books that parents may wish to review. Each is written in a clear, readable style; is of particular interest to parents of handicapped children; is readily available; has been read or used by other parents and professionals; and has received a positive review.

Dickerson MU: *Our Four Boys: Foster Parenting Retarded Teenagers.* Syracuse, NY, Syracuse University Press, 1979.

Perske R, Perske M: *Hope for the Families: New Directions for Parents of Persons with Retardation or Other Developmental Disabilities.* Nashville, Abingdon Press, 1981.

Turnbull AP, Turnbull HR: *Parents Speak Out: Then and Now.* Columbus, OH, Merrill Publishing Company, 1985.

White BL: *The First Three Years of Life.* Old Tappan, NJ, Simon & Schuster, 1985.

The following agencies may be contacted for printed materials and information regarding their services. Some may have state and/or local chapters.

American Association on Mental Deficiency (AAMD), 1719 Kalorama Road, N.W., Washington, DC 20009, (202) 387-1968.

American Speech-Language-Hearing Association (ASHA), 10801 Rockville Pike, Rockville, MD 20852, (301) 897-5700.

Association for Children and Adults with Learning Disabilities (ACALD), 4156 Library Road, Pittsburgh, PA 15234, (412) 341-1515.

Association for Retarded Citizens (ARC), P.O. Box 6109, Arlington, TX 76005, (817) 640-0204.

National Down Syndrome Congress, 1800 Dempster, Park Ridge, IL 60068-1146, (312) 823-7550.

National Down Syndrome Society (NDSS), 141 Fifth Avenue, New York, NY 10010, (800) 221-4602 or (212) 460-9330. (A public information packet, including a booklet, "This Baby Needs You Even More," a bibliography of up-to-date reading materials, and a state-by-state list of parent groups and early intervention programs, is available in both English and Spanish from the National Down Syndrome Society.)

Special Olympics (SO), 1350 New York Avenue, N.W., Suite 500, Washington, DC 20005, (202) 628-3630.

The Association for Persons with Severe Handicaps (TAPSH), 7010 Roosevelt Way, N.E., Seattle, WA 98115, (206) 523-8446.

State Mental Retardation Authorities

ALABAMA

Associate Commissioner for Mental Retardation
Department of Mental Health
200 Interstate Park Drive
Montgomery, Alabama 36109
(205) 271-9295

ALASKA

Program Administrator
Developmental Disabilities Section
Division of Mental Health and Developmental Disabilities
Department of Health and Social Services
P.O. Box H-04
Juneau, Alaska 99811
(907) 465-3372

ARIZONA

Assistant Director
Division of Developmental Disabilities
Department of Economic Security
P.O.Box 6760
Phoenix, Arizona 85005
(602) 255-5775

ARKANSAS

Deputy Director
Developmental Disabilities Services
Department of Human Services
Suite 400, Waldon Building
7th and Main Streets
Little Rock, Arkansas 72201
(501) 371-3419

CALIFORNIA

Director

Department of Developmental Services

Health and Welfare Agency

1600 9th Street, N.W., 2nd Floor

Sacramento, California 95814

(916) 323-3131

COLORADO

Director

Division for Developmental Disabilities

Department of Institutions

3824 West Princeton Circle

Denver, Colorado 80236

(303) 762-4550

CONNECTICUT

Commissioner

Department of Mental Retardation

90 Pitkin Street

East Hartford, Connecticut 06108

(203) 528-7141

DELAWARE

Director

Division of Mental Retardation

Department of Health and Social Services

449 North duPont Highway

Dover, Delaware 19901

(302) 736-4386

DISTRICT OF COLUMBIA

Administrator
Mental Retardation/Developmental Disabilities
Administration
Department of Human Services
Randall School Building, Room 200
1st and Eye Street, S.W.
Washington, DC 20024
(202) 727-5930

FLORIDA

Director
Developmental Services Program Office
Department of Health and Rehabilitative Services
1311 Winewood Blvd.
Building 5, Room 215
Tallahassee, Florida 32301
(904) 488-4257

GEORGIA

Deputy Director
Mental Retardation Services
Division of Mental Health and Mental Retardation
Department of Human Resources
878 Peachtree Street, N.E., Rm 304
Atlanta, Georgia 30309
(404) 894-6300

HAWAII

Executive Secretary
State Developmental Disabilities Planning and
Advisory Council
Department of Health
P.O.Box 3378
Honolulu, Hawaii 96801
(808) 548-8482 or 548-8483

IDAHO

Chief, Bureau of Developmental Disabilities
Division of Community Rehabilitation
Department of Health and Welfare
450 West State Street, 10th Floor
Boise, Idaho 83720
(208) 334-4181

ILLINOIS

Deputy Director for Developmental Disabilities
Department of Mental Health and Developmental Disabilities
402 Stratton Office Building
Springfield, Illinois 62706
(217) 782-7393

INDIANA

Director
Division of Developmental Disabilities
Department of Mental Health
117 East Washington
Indianapolis, Indiana 46204
(317) 232-7826

IOWA

Director
Division of Mental Health, Mental Retardation, and
Developmental Disabilities
Department of Human Services
Hoover State Office Building
Des Moines, Iowa 50319
(515) 281-6003

KANSAS

Director of Clinical Programs
Department of Social and Rehabilitation Services
State Office Building, 5th Floor
Topeka, Kansas 66612
(913) 296-3471

KENTUCKY

Director
Division of Mental Retardation
Department 4-Mental Health and Mental Retardation
275 East Main
Frankfort, Kentucky 40621
(502) 564-7700

LOUISIANA

Assistant Secretary
Office of Mental Retardation
Department of Health and Human Resources
721 Government Street, Room 308
Baton Rouge, Louisiana 70804
(504) 342-6811

MAINE

Director
Bureau of Mental Retardation
Department of Mental Health and Mental Retardation
Station 40 S.O.B.
Augusta, Maine 04333
(207) 289-3161

MARYLAND

Director
Mental Retardation and Developmental
Disabilities Administration
Department of Health and Mental Hygiene
201 West Preston Street
Baltimore, Maryland 21201
(301) 225 5600

MASSACHUSETTS

Commissioner for Mental Retardation
Department of Mental Health
160 North Washington Street
Boston, Massachusetts 02114
(617) 727-5608

MICHIGAN

Administrator
Bureau of Community Residential Services
Department of Mental Health
6th Floor, Lewis Cass Building
Lansing, Michigan 48926
(517) 373-2900

MINNESOTA

Director
Mental Retardation Division
Department of Human Services
Centennial Office Building
4th Floor
St. Paul, Minnesota 55155
(612) 296-2160

MISSISSIPPI

Director
Bureau of Mental Retardation
Department of Mental Health
1500 Woolfolk Building
Jackson, Mississippi 39201
(601) 359-1290

MISSOURI

Director
Division of Mental Retardation and
Developmental Disabilities
Department of Mental Health
2002 Missouri Blvd.
P.O.Box 687
Jefferson City, Missouri 65102
(314) 751-4054

MONTANA

Administrator
Developmental Disabilities Division
Department of Social and Rehabilitation Services
P.O.Box 4210
Helena, Montana 59604
(406) 444-2995

NEBRASKA

Director
Office of Mental Retardation
Department of Public Institutions
P.O.Box 94728
Lincoln, Nebraska 68509
(402) 471-2851

NEVADA

Associate Administrator
Division of Mental Health and Mental Retardation
Department of Human Resources
1001 North Mountain Street
Gilbert Building, Suite 1-H
Carson City, Nevada 89710
(702) 885-5943

NEW HAMPSHIRE

Deputy Director
Division of Mental Health and Developmental Services
Department of Health and Human Services
Health and Human Services Building
Hazen Drive
Concord, New Hampshire 03301
(603) 271-4728

NEW JERSEY

Director
Division of Mental Retardation
Department of Human Services
222 South Warren Street
Capitol Place One
Trenton, New Jersey 08625
(609) 292-3742

NEW MEXICO

Director
Behavioral Health Services Division
Health and Environment Department
P.O.Box 968
Santa Fe, New Mexico 87504-0968
(505) 827-2660

NEW YORK

Commissioner
Office of Mental Retardation and Developmental Disabilities
44 Holland Avenue
Albany, New York 12229
(518) 473-1997

NORTH CAROLINA

Director for Mental Retardation

Division of Mental Health/Mental Retardation and

Substance Abuse Services

Department of Human Services

325 North Salisbury Street

Raleigh, North Carolina 27611

(919) 733-3654 or 733-7011

NORTH DAKOTA

Director

Developmental Disabilities Division

Department of Human Services

State Capitol Building

Bismarck, North Dakota 58505

(701) 224-2768

OHIO

Director

Department of Mental Retardation and

Developmental Disabilities

State Office Tower

30 East Broad Street

Room 1284

Columbus, Ohio 43215

(614) 466-5214

OKLAHOMA

Assistant Director

Developmental Disabilities

Department of Human Services

P.O.Box 25352

Oklahoma City, Oklahoma 73125

(405) 521-3571

OREGON

Assistant Administrator
Program for Mental Retardation and Developmental Disabilities
Division of Mental Health
Department of Human Resources
2575 Bittern Street, N.W.
Salem, Oregon 97310
(503) 378-2429

PENNSYLVANIA

Deputy Secretary for Mental Retardation
Department of Public Welfare
Room 302, Health and Welfare Building
Harrisburg, Pennsylvania 17120
(717) 787-3700

PUERTO RICO

Assistant Secretary for Family Services
Department of Social Services
P.O.Box 11398
Santurce, Puerto Rico 00910
(809) 723-2127

RHODE ISLAND

Executive Director
Division of Retardation
Department of MHRH
Aime J.Forand Building
600 New London Avenue
Cranston, Rhode Island 02920
(401) 464-3234

SOUTH CAROLINA

Commissioner
Department of Mental Retardation
2712 Middleburg Drive
P.O.Box 4706
Columbia, South Carolina 29240
(803) 737-6474

SOUTH DAKOTA

Program Administrator
Office of Developmental Disabilities and Mental Health
Department of Social Services
Kneip Building
Pierre, South Dakota 57501
(605) 773-3438

TENNESSEE

Assistant Commissioner for Mental Retardation
Department of Mental Health and Mental Retardation
James K. Polk State Office Building
505 Deaderick Street
Nashville, Tennessee 37219
(615) 741-3803

TEXAS

Deputy Commissioner for Mental Retardation Services
Department of Mental Health and Mental Retardation
Box 12668
Austin, Texas 78711-2668
(512) 465-4520

UTAH

Director

Division of Services to the Handicapped

Department of Social Services

150 West NorthTemple, 4th Floor

P.O.Box 2500

Salt Lake City, Utah 84110

(801) 533-4940

VERMONT

Director of Mental Retardation Programs

Department of Mental Health

103 South Main Street

Waterbury, Vermont 05676

(802) 241-2636

VIRGINIA

Commissioner

Department of Mental Health and Mental Retardation

109 Governor Street

P.O. Box 1797

James Madison Building, 13th Floor

Richmond, Virginia 23214

(804) 786-4982

WASHINGTON

Director

Division of Developmental Disabilities

Department of Social and Health Services

P.O.Box 1788, OB-42C

Olympia, Washington 98504

(206) 753-3900

WEST VIRGINIA

Director, Developmental Disabilities Services
Division of Behavioral Health
Department of Health
1800 Washington Street, East
Charleston, West Virginia 25305
(304) 348-0627

WISCONSIN

Director
Developmental Disabilities Office
Bureau of Community Services
Department of Health and Social Services
P.O.Box 7851
Madison, Wisconsin 53707
(608) 266-2862

WYOMING

Executive Secretary
Board of Charities and Reform
Herschler Building, 1st Floor West
Cheyenne, Wyoming 82002
(307) 777-7405

For further information, contact:

Robert Gettings
Executive Director
National Association of State Mental Retardation Programs
113 Oronoco Street
Alexandria, Virginia 22314
(703) 683-4202